5 ingredients

ingredients

no... nom nom

CHINESE

takeaway kitchen

🍎 CookNation

5 INGREDIENTS nom nom CHINESE TAKEAWAY KITCHEN

YOUR FAVOURITE CHINESE TAKEAWAY DISHES AT HOME. QUICK & EASY.

Copyright © Bell & Mackenzie Publishing Limited 2019

ISBN 978-1-913174-04-0

DISCLAIMER

CookNation

BELL & MACKENZIE
PUBLISHING LIMITED

www.bellmackenzie.com

CONTENTS

VEGETABLES 51

MEAT/POULTRY/SEAFOOD 67

CONVERSION CHART 95

INTRODUCTION

Cooking Chinese food at home, nom nom-style, is much easier than you think, plus it's cheaper and can be a better choice nutritionally than your local takeaway.

Who doesn't love a good takeaway? Chinese cuisine is one of the nation's favourite meals, with an enormous range of delicious dishes bursting with flavour and satisfying cravings up and down the country. Ordering takeaway on a regular basis can of course be expensive, and deep down, we all know that it isn't always the healthiest! The good news is, cooking Chinese food at home, nom nom-style, is much easier than you think, plus it's cheaper and can be a better choice nutritionally than your local takeaway.

In Chinese culture food is an important part of life, demanding respect and giving pleasure, whether dining alone, with friends, loved ones or family. Every mouthful should be savoured, allowing your taste buds to delight in the diverse array of flavours - sweet, sour, hot or salty.

The Chinese takeaway-style of food, and the taste you are probably most familiar with, is traditional Cantonese meals, originating from Guangdong, China. The delights of Cantonese cooking have spread like wildfire across the West, winning the hearts and stomachs of so many Brits and Americans.

Many people have the misconception that all Chinese food is difficult to cook; complex ingredients, methods and unfamiliar utensils, making it a non-starter. Think again! Our mouth-watering selection of favourite traditional Chinese dishes are genuinely simple to recreate - with just 5 ingredients.

As with many cuisines, there are, of course, some staple ingredients that form the base of so many dishes that are both invaluable and essential items for your kitchen store cupboard. With this in mind, our nom nom selection of Chinese recipes are simple: all recipes require no more than 5 additional ingredients! Naturally, creating Chinese takeaway-style recipes with just 5 ingredients requires some pre-prepared/cheat items such a jar of ready-made sweet & sour sauce, but there are plenty of recipes that are made entirely from scratch.

5 Simple Ingredients + Store Cupboard Essentials = nom nom Chinese Takeaway

By pairing 5 (or less) simple supermarket ingredients with some store cupboard essentials like garlic, soy sauce and sesame oil, you'll be enjoying takeaway-style meals in minutes.

You may already have many of the core ingredients in your kitchen cupboards, but cross-reference against the following list of must-haves. With these underpinning, basic ingredients in stock, you'll be ready to whip up

Chinese takeaway, **nom nom**-style, any day of the week. We use foods that you can easily source from any UK supermarket, but still bring incredible flavour to the dish.

·············· STORE CUPBOARD INGREDIENTS ··············

- Vegetable Oil
- Sesame Oil
- Soy Sauce
- Salt & Pepper
- Brown Sugar
- Garlic
- Cider Vinegar
- Rice Vinegar
- Fish Sauce

- Baking Powder
- Tomato Ketchup
- Tomato Puree
- Plain Flour
- Cornflour
- Oyster Sauce
- Chinese Five Spice Powder
- Hoisin Sauce

As with all of our recipes, feel free to adapt with the ingredients, portions, ratios and techniques to suit your preferences. There are no strict guidelines - just enjoy cooking the Nom Nom way and allow yourself to be led through these delicious takeaway-style specialities - with just 5 simple ingredients. Build confidence in the kitchen by adding your own twist to suit your, diet and taste buds.

To make your **nom nom** cooking experience even simpler, it's a good idea to own a good quality wok. This will improve your cooking and needn't cost the Earth.

A good quality wok is a great investment. A large frying pan can serve as an alternative, however you cannot mimic the ease of cooking with a wok, with its deep sides and heavy base, for a wide range of cooking methods. You may just associate a wok with stir-frying, however it's far more versatile than that and can be used for everything from steaming to soup making. Love your wok, look after your wok! Many Chinese chefs would insist that you do not wash your wok! After cooking, rinse your wok under warm water to clean and then pat before storing. You will then find that your wok builds up a coat of delicious seasoning which is a critically important traditional method of enhancing taste and adding vital flavour while cooking.

We hope you enjoy cooking our **nom nom** Chinese takeaway-style dishes at home.

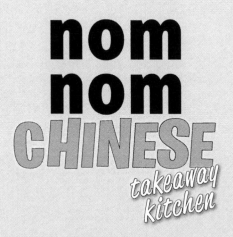

APPETISERS/STARTERS/SOUPS

BBQ SPARE RIBS

5 Ingredients

- 1 tsp honey
- 4 Asian shallots, peeled and finely chopped
- 3 tsp English mustard
- 800g/1¾lbs pork spare ribs
- 2 tsp sesame seeds

Method

1 To make the marinade, mix the honey, shallots and mustard in a bowl with 1 freshly minced clove of garlic.

2 Pour in 4 teaspoons of soy sauce and 6 tablespoons of hoisin sauce and mix thoroughly together.

3 Add the ribs and rub the marinade in well.

4 Cover the bowl and place in the refrigerator for 30-60 minutes - the longer the better.

5 Meanwhile, pre-heat the oven to 200C/400F/Gas 6.

6 Remove the ribs from the bowl and place them onto a roasting tray.

7 Pour any remaining marinade over the ribs.

8 Cook in the oven for 45 minutes, or until cooked through.

9 To serve, place on a dish and sprinkle over the sesame seeds.

WHAT YOU'LL NEED FROM YOUR STORE CUPBOARD
•garlic•soy sauce•hoisin sauce

DRY BBQ SPARE RIBS

5 Ingredients

- 1 tsp honey
- 4 Asian shallots
- 3 tsp English mustard
- 800g/1¾lbs pork spare ribs
- A wedge of lemon

Method

1 To make the marinade, mix the honey, shallots and mustard in a bowl with 1 freshly minced clove of garlic.

2 Pour in 4 teaspoons of soy sauce and 6 tablespoons of hoisin sauce and mix thoroughly together.

3 Add the ribs and rub the marinade in well.

4 Cover the bowl and place in the refrigerator for 30 minutes.

5 Meanwhile, pre-heat the oven to 200C/400F/Gas 6.

6 Remove the marinated ribs from the fridge and take each rib out of the bowl. Allow as much of the marinade as possible to slide off.

7 Pat dry with a kitchen towel and then arrange on greaseproof paper on a roasting tray.

8 Cook in the oven for 35-40 minutes, or until cooked through.

9 Serve with a wedge of lemon.

WHAT YOU'LL NEED FROM YOUR STORE CUPBOARD
•garlic•soy sauce•hoisin sauce

SWEET AND SOUR SPARE RIBS

nom

5 Ingredients

- 50g/2oz onion, roughly chopped
- 75g/3oz red pepper, de-seeded and chopped
- 75g/3oz yellow pepper, de-seeded and chopped
- 1 tin of pineapple
- 800g/1¾lbs pork spare ribs

Method

1 Pre-heat the oven to 200C/400F/Gas 6 and then begin by making the sweet and sour sauce. Add into a small bowl one tablespoon of cornflour and 1 tablespoon of water. Whisk together well and set aside.

2 Place a wok on a medium heat and drizzle in a little sesame oil. Once hot, add in the chopped onion and peppers and cook for 2-3 minutes.

3 Drain and retain the juice of the pineapple. Chop into chunks.

4 Add the pineapple chunks and juice into the wok along with 75ml/2½floz of rice vinegar, 75g/3oz of brown sugar, 1 tablespoon of soy sauce and 3 tablespoons of tomato ketchup, then bring to a boil.

5 Add in 1 tablespoon of the cornflour mixture and mix well.

6 Cook for 2 minutes, stirring occasionally, until the sauce thickens.

7 Place the ribs in a roasting dish and pour over the sweet and sour sauce. Cook in the oven for 45 minutes, or until cooked through. Serve immediately whilst still warm.

WHAT YOU'LL NEED FROM YOUR STORE CUPBOARD
•rice vinegar•brown sugar•soy sauce•tomato ketchup•cornflour

FISH KEBABS WITH SWEET CHILLI SAUCE

nom

5 Ingredients

- 225g/8oz tuna steak, diced
- 225g/8oz large prawns, peeled and de-veined
- 1 red bell pepper, de-seeded and diced
- ½ courgette, diced
- Sweet chilli sauce for dipping

Method

1 Pre-heat the grill to a high heat and combine all of the main ingredients in a bowl.

2 In a separate bowl, mix a large splash of olive oil, 1 freshly minced clove of garlic and a pinch of salt and pepper.

3 Add the oil mixture to the bowl containing the fish and vegetables.

4 Turn the fish and vegetables well in the oil to evenly coat them and leave to rest for 5-10 minutes.

5 Next, thread the ingredients onto metal skewers, alternating between fish and vegetables, and place them under grill.

6 Watch them and turn as they cook through for around 3-4 minutes each side, ensuring the tuna begins to brown and the prawns go pink.

7 Serve straight from the grill with a sweet chilli dipping sauce.

WHAT YOU'LL NEED FROM YOUR STORE CUPBOARD
•olive oil•garlic•salt & pepper

TOFU NOODLE SOUP

nom

5 Ingredients

- 600ml/1 pint vegetable stock
- 1 small piece of ginger, peeled and chopped
- 125g/4oz tofu, diced
- 225g/8oz pak choi, chopped
- 100g/3½oz soba noodles

Method

1 Take two large saucepans; fill one two thirds full of water and place on the hob to boil, and pour the vegetable stock into the other.

2 Add 3 freshly minced cloves of garlic to the vegetable stock along with the ginger, tofu and a dash of soy sauce.

3 Bring the pan to boil and allow to simmer for 10 minutes.

4 Next, add in the pak choi and simmer for a further 2-3 minutes.

5 Meanwhile, in the first pan, cook the noodles for around 1 minute if fresh, or 4-5 minutes if dried.

6 Once cooked, drain the noodles and add to bowls.

7 To serve, pour the tofu soup over the noodles.

WHAT YOU'LL NEED FROM YOUR STORE CUPBOARD
•garlic•soy sauce

STIR-FRIED GREENS

5 Ingredients

- A splash of fresh lime juice
- 100g/3½oz pak choi, leaves stripped and sliced
- 125g/4oz Chinese cabbage, shredded
- 75g/3oz mangetout
- 1 small courgette, diced

Method

1 First, wash the vegetables and dry before frying.

2 Heat a wok over a medium heat and add a in a drizzle of sesame oil.

3 Then, add in a good dash of soy sauce, followed by a squeeze of fresh lime juice and a pinch of sugar, stirring with a wooden spoon.

4 Add the pak choi and Chinese cabbage into the wok and cook for 1 minute before adding in the mangetout, stir and allow to cook for a further minute, and then add in the courgette. Stir rapidly to coat and cook the vegetables, adding a bit of extra soy towards the end.

5 Once cooked, place in a bowl and serve whilst warm.

WHAT YOU'LL NEED FROM YOUR STORE CUPBOARD
•sesame oil•soy sauce•brown sugar

SESAME PRAWNS ON TOAST

5 Ingredients

- 200g/7oz king prawns, peeled and de-veined
- 1 egg white
- 2 tsp fresh ginger, finely chopped
- 4 slices of white bread, crusts removed
- 4 tbsp sesame seeds

Method

1 Add the prawns, egg white, 1 tsp soy sauce, salt pepper and ginger into a food processor and blitz until you have a lumpy paste.

2 Meanwhile, cut the slices of bread into triangles.

3 Evenly spread the prawn mixture over the bread triangles - try to get a layer that has a thickness of around ½cm.

4 Then, add a generous layer of sesame seeds on top.

5 In a medium sized saucepan, heat around 2cm of vegetable oil for frying.

6 In batches, fry the prawn toasts by first lowering them in prawn-side down for 2 minutes, then flip them and fry for a further 2 minutes, until golden and crispy.

7 Remove the toast using a slotted spoon and place on kitchen paper to remove excess oil. Plate immediately and serve whilst hot.

WHAT YOU'LL NEED FROM YOUR STORE CUPBOARD
•soy sauce•salt & pepper•vegetable oil

DUCK SPRING ROLLS

5 Ingredients

- 2 duck breasts, thinly sliced
- 250g/9oz bell peppers, deseeded and finely sliced
- 1 carrot, grated
- 175g/6oz beansprouts
- 4 spring roll sheets

Method

1 Place a wok or saucepan on medium-high heat with a splash of sesame oil and add the duck.

2 Once the fat starts to render, use a slotted spoon to remove the duck and place to one side. Add some more sesame oil to the wok, then add the peppers, carrot and a teaspoon of soy sauce.

3 Stir-fry for 2-3 minutes, then add in the duck, beansprouts, a crushed clove of garlic and 2 tablespoons hoisin sauce, and fry until the duck is cooked through.

4 Once cooked, mix well and place in a bowl.

5 Next, heat a large pot of oil, or a deep fat fryer, to 180C/350F.

6 Meanwhile, spoon the stir-fried mixture into the centre of each spring roll wrapper and roll up, making sure you tuck in the ends.

7 Deep-fry the spring rolls until golden brown, remove with a slotted spoon and place on some kitchen roll to remove any excess oil.

8 Serve the rolls immediately whilst warm.

WHAT YOU'LL NEED FROM YOUR STORE CUPBOARD
•sesame oil•soy sauce•garlic•hoisin sauce

VEGETABLE SPRING ROLLS

5 Ingredients

- 250g/9oz mixed bell peppers, de-seeded and finely sliced
- 2 carrots, peeled and grated
- 175g/6oz beansprouts
- 1 spring onion, finely sliced
- 4 spring roll sheets

Method

1 Place a wok on a medium-high heat and add in a splash of vegetable oil. Add in the mixed peppers and stir fry for 1-2 minutes, stirring regularly.

2 Add in the carrots, beansprouts, spring onion and a freshly minced clove of garlic, along with a good splash of soy sauce, and cook for a further 2-3 minutes, until the vegetables are beginning to soften.

3 Once cooked, remove from the wok and place the mixed vegetables in a bowl to one side while you heat a large pot of oil, or a deep fat fryer, to 180C/350F.

4 Meanwhile, spoon the stir-fried mixture into the centre of each spring roll wrapper and roll up, making sure you tuck in the ends.

5 Carefully place each roll to one side, ready to cook once the oil is boiling.

6 Deep-fry the spring rolls in the oil until golden brown, then remove with a slotted spoon. Place on some kitchen roll to remove any excess oil, dabbing the spring roll all over.

7 Serve the rolls immediately and enjoy warm.

WHAT YOU'LL NEED FROM YOUR STORE CUPBOARD
•vegetable oil•garlic•soy sauce

GARLIC AND CHILLI PRAWNS

5 Ingredients

- 300g/10oz fresh prawns, peeled and de-veined.
- 1 tsp chilli flakes
- 1 tbsp sesame seeds
- 2 spring onions, finely chopped

Method

1 Place a wok on a high heat and add in a drizzle of sesame oil.

2 Fry the prawns for 2–3 minutes, or until lightly golden, and then transfer onto a plate.

3 Reduce the heat to medium and add in a splash more sesame oil.

4 Add in 2 cloves of freshly minced garlic, along with the chilli flakes, and fry until the garlic softens.

5 Then, add in 120ml/4floz of water, 2 teaspoons of soy sauce and 2 tablespoons of sugar, and simmer for 3-4 minutes, or until the sauce begins to thicken to a syrup-like consistency.

6 Place the prawns back into the saucepan to reheat and toss to coat them evenly in the sauce.

7 Once cooked, place the prawns on a serving dish and scatter with the chopped spring onions.

WHAT YOU'LL NEED FROM YOUR STORE CUPBOARD

•sesame oil•garlic•soy sauce•brown sugar

CHICKEN SATAY STICKS

5 Ingredients

- 1 small piece of ginger, peeled and grated
- 1 tsp clear honey
- 3 tbsp smooth peanut butter
- 500g/1lb 2oz chicken breasts, chopped
- 150ml/5floz coconut milk

Method

1 To make the marinade, combine the grated ginger, 2 crushed cloves of garlic, honey, 1 tablespoon of soy sauce and peanut butter in a bowl.

2 Mix well, and if the sauce is a little thick, add a splash of water.

3 Set the marinade aside ready to use shortly.

4 Place each chicken breast into a freezer bag and flatten using a rolling pin.

5 Once flattened, cut the chicken into strips and coat in 1/3 of the satay marinade. Cover and place in the fridge until required.

6 Meanwhile, place the remaining satay marinade into a saucepan over low heat and combine with the coconut milk. Gently heat and stir.

7 Pre-heat the grill to a high heat.

8 Take the marinated chicken and thread the chunks onto metal skewers.

9 Place the skewers onto a baking tray brushed with sesame oil and grill for around 10 minutes ,until slightly charred, turning often.

10 Serve immediately on a platter, drizzling the satay sauce over the skewers.

WHAT YOU'LL NEED FROM YOUR STORE CUPBOARD
•garlic•soy sauce•sesame oil

CRUNCHY PEANUT PRAWN SKEWERS

nom

5 Ingredients

- 1 small piece of ginger, peeled and grated
- 1 tsp clear honey
- 3 tbsp smooth peanut butter
- 500g/1lb 2oz fresh prawns, de-shelled
- 1 tbsp peanuts, crushed

Method

1 Begin by preparing the marinade. Add the grated ginger and 2 freshly minced cloves of garlic into a bowl, along with the honey and peanut butter, then pour in 1 tablespoon of soy sauce.

2 Mix well - if the sauce is a little thick, a splash of water can be added.

3 Add the prawns into the marinade, ensuring they are evenly covered, and leave to marinade for 15-20 minutes.

4 Pre-heat the grill to a high heat.

5 Sprinkle the crushed peanuts into the prawn satay marinade mixture and stir well.

6 Thread the prawns onto skewers. Place the skewers onto a baking tray brushed with oil and grill for 3-4 minutes, before removing from the grill. Turn the skewers over and return to the grill for a further 3-4 minutes to cook on the other side.

7 Repeat again for a shorter length of time on each side if the prawns are not yet cooked through.

8 On the final turn, drizzle any of the remaining marinade over the skewers, or warm through in a small pan to use as a dip.

9 Serve straight from the grill whilst warm.

WHAT YOU'LL NEED FROM YOUR STORE CUPBOARD
•garlic •soy sauce•sesame oil

21

CUCUMBER SALAD

5 Ingredients

- 2 large cucumbers
- 2 tbsp white wine vinegar
- 1 sprig of coriander leaves, roughly chopped
- A handful of peanuts, crushed

Method

1 Using a peeler ,make fine cucumber ribbons until you get to the seeds.

2 To make the salad dressing, combine the white wine vinegar with a tsp of sugar until it dissolves. Toss the cucumber ribbons with the dressing and add in the coriander.

3 To serve, scatter the crushed peanuts over the salad.

WHAT YOU'LL NEED FROM YOUR STORE CUPBOARD
•brown sugar

PRAWN CRACKERS

5 Ingredients

- 500g/1lb 2oz fresh prawns, peeled and de-veined
- 500g/1lb 2oz tapioca flour
- 1 tsp cayenne pepper
- 1 tsp baking powder

Method

1 In a food processor, blitz the prawns to a fine paste. Mix in the tapioca flour and continue to blitz until you get a thick dough.

2 Next, add in a pinch of salt and pepper ,along with the cayenne pepper and baking powder - mix thoroughly. Knead the dough until it is smooth, you may need to add a splash of water or a bit more flour depending on the texture of your dough.

3 Then, split the dough in two and shape into log shaped rolls that will fit inside your steamer.

4 Bring a saucepan of water with a single steamer to the boil, add in the rolls and steam for around 60 minutes.

5 Remove from the steamer and allow to cool - at this point they should have a rubber-like texture.

6 Using a sharp knife cut thin slices from the rolls and dry them.

7 Once dry, bring a saucepan containing around 2cm of oil to the boil and deep fry your prawn crackers – they may need to be held down in the oil.

8 Remove from the oil using a slotted spoon and place on a kitchen towel to removed excess oil. To serve, immediately place them in a bowl with dipping sauces of your choice.

WHAT YOU'LL NEED FROM YOUR STORE CUPBOARD
- salt & pepper • vegetable oil

CRISPY SEAWEED

nom

5 Ingredients

- 300g kale, sliced and dried

Method

1 Pre-heat a wok over high heat and add 200ml/7floz of sesame oil.

2 Add around a quarter of the kale into the hot oil and cook for a couple of minutes, until it is crispy. Remove using a slotted spoon and place the kale onto kitchen paper to get rid of any excess oil.

3 Repeat this method in batches with the rest of the kale

4 Pour away any excess oil from the wok and place all of the crispy kale back in.

5 Season using half a teaspoon of Chinese five-spice powder, a pinch of sugar and half a teaspoon of salt.

6 Mix everything together, ensuring and even coating and serve in a bowl to enjoy warm.

WHAT YOU'LL NEED FROM YOUR STORE CUPBOARD
•sesame oil•Chinese 5 spice powder•brown sugar•salt

HOT AND SOUR SOUP

nom

5 Ingredients

- 400g/14oz tinned chicken broth
- 225g/8oz soft tofu, diced
- 175g/6oz button mushrooms, sliced
- 1 egg, beaten
- 1 tsp chilli oil

Method

1 Add 2 tablespoons of cornflour to 3 tablespoons of water and mix until dissolved. Set this aside to use shortly.

2 Meanwhile, pre-heat a saucepan over a medium heat.

3 Once warm, add in the chicken broth and bring to boil.

4 Stir in the tofu and mushrooms and simmer for 2 minutes.

5 Next, add 3 tablespoons of soy sauce, 2 tablespoons of rice vinegar and a pinch of pepper, and mix well.

6 Pour in the cornflour mixture and stir continuously until the soup thickens.

7 Remove from the heat. Then, add in the beaten eggs and swirl using chopsticks until egg threads form.

8 To serve, pour immediately into bowls and drizzle with a bit of chilli oil.

WHAT YOU'LL NEED FROM YOUR STORE CUPBOARD
•soy sauce•rice vinegar•black pepper

CHICKEN NOODLE SOUP

nom

5 Ingredients

- 4 celery sticks, sliced
- 2 litres/3 pints chicken stock
- 225g/8oz chicken breast, cooked and chopped
- 60g/2½ fine egg noodles
- 150g/5oz carrots, sliced

Method

1 Pre-heat a large saucepan over medium heat and add 2 tablespoons of sesame oil.

2 Add in the celery and cook for 4-5 minutes, or until tender.

3 Next, add the chicken stock, chicken chunks, noodles, carrots, 2 teaspoons of sugar, 4 tablespoons of soy sauce and a pinch of salt and pepper.

4 Bring the pan to the boil, then lower the heat and allow to simmer for 20 minutes before serving equally between bowls.

WHAT YOU'LL NEED FROM YOUR STORE CUPBOARD
•brown sugar•soy sauce•salt & pepper

CRAB AND SWEETCORN SOUP

nom

5 Ingredients

- 300g/10½oz canned sweetcorn, drained
- 4 spring onions, finely sliced
- 200g/7oz crab meat
- 1 litre/1 pint 15floz of chicken stock
- 1 egg, beaten

Method

1 In a food processor or blender, add around three-quarters of the sweetcorn and blitz until smooth.

2 Meanwhile, heat a saucepan over a medium heat and add a tablespoon of vegetable oil.

3 Stir-fry most of the spring onion until softened.

4 Add the puréed sweetcorn, crab meat and chicken stock and bring to the boil.

5 Reduce the heat and allow to simmer for 5 minutes.

6 Mix a teaspoon of cornflour with a little bit of water to make a paste and add this to the soup, stirring often until the soup thickens a little.

7 Next, add in the beaten eggs and swirl using chopsticks until egg threads form.

8 To serve, pour equal amounts into bowls and garnish with a scattering of any remaining spring onion.

WHAT YOU'LL NEED FROM YOUR STORE CUPBOARD
•vegetable oil

CHICKEN AND MUSHROOM SOUP

nom

5 Ingredients

- 200g/7oz chicken breast, finely chopped
- 200g/7oz button mushrooms, chopped
- 4 spring onions, finely sliced
- 1 litre/1 pint 15floz of chicken stock
- 1 egg, beaten

Method

1 Place a wok on a medium heat and drizzle in a good splash of vegetable oil.

2 Add in the sliced chicken and cook for 2-3 minutes, stirring regularly.

3 Once the chicken is sealed and mostly cooked through, add in the mushrooms and spring onion and cook for a further 2-3 minutes

4 Meanwhile, bring the stock to a boil, then reduce to a simmer.

5 Add in the chicken and mushroom mixture from the wok and simmer for 8-10 minutes.

6 Mix a teaspoon of cornflour with a little bit of water to make a paste and add this to the soup, stirring often until the soup thickens a little.

7 Next, add in the beaten egg and swirl using chopsticks until egg threads form. Simmer for a further 2-3 minutes, then serve in bowls with any remaining spring onion used to garnish.

WHAT YOU'LL NEED FROM YOUR STORE CUPBOARD
- vegetable oil

nom nom
CHINESE
takeaway kitchen

RICE & NOODLES

EGG NOODLES WITH CHINESE BROCCOLI

nom

5 Ingredients

- 150g/5oz fresh egg noodles
- 3 Asian shallots, peeled & finely chopped
- 4 sprigs Chinese broccoli
- 2 sprigs kale

Method

1 Bring a saucepan of water to the boil and blanch the egg noodles for 1 minute.

2 Drain the noodles, rinse with hot water and then place on a serving dish.

3 Meanwhile, combine 2 tablespoons of soy sauce, a splash of cider vinegar, and a tablespoon of sugar.

4 Place a saucepan or wok on a medium heat with some sesame oil and fry the shallots until brown.

5 Stir in the soy mixture, remove from the heat and pour over the noodles, tossing everything together.

6 Put the broccoli and kale in a bowl, cover with boiling water and blanch for around 1 minute.

Drain and then place on top of the noodles.

7 To serve, season with a dash of sesame or chilli oil.

WHAT YOU'LL NEED FROM YOUR STORE CUPBOARD
•soy sauce•cider vinegar•brown sugar•sesame oil•chilli oil

RICE NOODLES WITH CRISPY BEEF

5 Ingredients

- 1 tsp honey
- 1 tbsp peanuts, crushed
- 200g/7oz lean minced beef
- 150g/5oz rice noodles
- 2 spring onions, chopped

Method

1 Place a frying pan on a medium heat and add a dash of sesame oil.

2 Add in 1 clove of freshly minced garlic, along with the honey and peanuts, shortly followed by the minced beef, and stir-fry for 5 minutes, or until the mince is golden brown and crisp.

3 Meanwhile, crush another clove of garlic and combine with 1 teaspoon of soy sauce and 1 teaspoon of oyster sauce to make a dressing.

4 Cook the rice noodles according the to the packet instructions, drain and place on a serving plate.

5 To serve, scatter the crispy beef and chopped spring onions over the noodles and drizzle over the dressing.

WHAT YOU'LL NEED FROM YOUR STORE CUPBOARD
•sesame oil•garlic•oyster sauce

31

STIR-FRIED BEEF AND PHO NOODLES

5 Ingredients

- 200g/7oz sirloin or rump steak, thinly sliced
- 125g/4oz mangetout
- ½ onion, chopped
- 400g/14oz fresh pho noodles
- 75g/3oz beansprouts

Method

1 Place a wok on a high heat and add a dash of oil.

2 Add in the steak strips and allow a minute to seal, before adding in the mangetout. Stir well and pour in 2 tablespoons of soy sauce and 1 tablespoon of oyster sauce.

3 Season with pepper and a clove of freshly minced garlic.

4 Stir once more and allow the mixture to cook for a further 2 minutes, stirring regularly, until the beef is thoroughly cooked through, or is at least browned and cooked to your preference.

5 Then, transfer the contents to a plate, allowing to rest.

6 Add the onion and noodles into the wok, along with another dash of soy and oyster sauce. Stir-fry for a couple of minutes, then add in the beansprouts, frying for a further minute. Once the noodles are cooked, serve immediately on a plate and place the steak and vegetables over the top.

WHAT YOU'LL NEED FROM YOUR STORE CUPBOARD

•vegetable oil•soy sauce•oyster sauce•black pepper•garlic

VEGETABLE CHOW MEIN

SERVES 2

5 Ingredients

- 225g/8oz yellow Chinese egg noodles
- ½ onion, chopped
- 1 medium carrot, grated
- ½ red bell pepper, de-seeded and sliced
- ½ head of broccoli, cut into florets

Method

1 Bring a saucepan of water to the boil and cook the egg noodles according to the packet instructions.

2 Once cooked, rinse, drain and set aside.

3 Meanwhile, in a bowl, mix together 2 tablespoons of soy sauce, 2 tablespoons of oyster sauce, 1 tablespoon of hoisin sauce and 2 tablespoons of water.

4 Place a wok on a high heat and add in a drizzle of vegetable oil.

5 Stir in 2 crushed garlic cloves and the chopped onion, and cook for 2-3 minutes, until soft. Next, add in the carrot, bell peppers and broccoli.

6 Stir-fry for 4-5 minutes, or until the vegetables are just cooked.

7 Add the noodles and sauce to the vegetables, toss everything together, and heat through for 2-3 minutes before serving straight from the wok.

WHAT YOU'LL NEED FROM YOUR STORE CUPBOARD

•soy sauce•oyster sauce•hoisin sauce•garlic•vegetable oil

BEEF CHOW MEIN

nom

5 Ingredients

- 225g/8oz Chinese yellow noodles
- 350g/12oz beef steak, thinly sliced
- ½ onion, chopped
- 1 red bell pepper, thinly sliced
- 75g/3oz frozen peas

Method

1 First, bring a saucepan of water to the boil and cook the noodles according to the packet instructions.

2 Meanwhile, mix together 2 tablespoons of soy sauce, 3 tablespoons of oyster sauce and 2 tablespoons of water.

3 Place a wok or frying pan on a high heat and add in a drizzle of vegetable oil. Place the strips of beef into the pan, season with a pinch of salt and black pepper, and fry for 2 minutes, until browned.

4 Once cooked, drain the noodles, rinse and place to one side.

5 Simultaneously, remove the cooked beef and set aside on a plate.

6 Add a splash more oil into the wok. Crush 2 cloves of garlic and add into the wok along with the onion, pepper and peas. Stir-fry for 2-3 minutes, until tender.

7 Next, return the beef and its juices to the wok, followed by the noodles and the chow mein sauce.

8 Toss everything together and heat through for 2 minutes, before serving whilst still hot.

WHAT YOU'LL NEED FROM YOUR STORE CUPBOARD
•soy sauce•oyster sauce•vegetable oil•salt & pepper•garlic

CHICKEN CHOW MEIN

nom

5 Ingredients

- 1 large chicken breast, thinly sliced
- 225g/8oz yellow Chinese egg noodles
- ½ onion, chopped
- 60g/2½oz bamboo shoots
- 1 medium carrot, grated

Method

1 Begin by preparing the chow mein marinade; In a bowl mix together 2 tablespoons of soy sauce, 2 tablespoons of oyster sauce, 1 tablespoon of hoisin and 2 tablespoons of water. Add in the sliced chicken and stir well to coat. Cover and leave for 15-20 minutes.

2 Bring a saucepan of water to the boil and cook the egg noodles according to the packet instructions.

3 Once cooked, rinse, drain and place to one side ready to use shortly.

4 Place a wok on a high heat and add in a drizzle of vegetable oil.

5 Crush 2 cloves of garlic into the wok, then add in the chopped onion.

6 Stir well and add in the marinated chicken, along with any excess marinade, closely followed by the bamboo shoots and carrot.

7 Stir-fry for 5-6 minutes, or until the chicken is completely cooked through.

8 Add in the cooked noodles, toss everything together, and warm through for 2-3 minutes before serving straight from the wok.

WHAT YOU'LL NEED FROM YOUR STORE CUPBOARD

•soy sauce•oyster sauce•hoisin sauce•vegetable oil•garlic

EGG FRIED RICE

nom

5 Ingredients

- 150g/5½oz long grain rice
- 2 large eggs, beaten
- ½ red pepper, thinly sliced
- 60g/2½oz peas
- 2 spring onions, thinly sliced

Method

1 Pour 300ml/10floz of water into a saucepan and bring to the boil.

2 Reduce the heat and add in the rice, cover with a lid, and cook for 10 minutes, unless the packet instructions state otherwise.

3 Once cooked, remove from the heat, drain and set aside to cool.

4 Meanwhile, pre-heat a wok or frying pan over medium heat and add a splash of sesame oil. Add in the eggs and cook until scrambled, stirring often with a spatula.

5 Remove the eggs from the pan and place onto a plate.

6 Add a splash more oil into the pan, then fry 2 freshly minced cloves of garlic and the red pepper for 2 minutes, seasoning with a pinch of salt and pepper.

7 Next, add the cooked rice, peas, most of the spring onion, scrambled egg and 2 tablespoons of soy sauce, and cook for 4-5 minutes, stirring continuously.

8 To serve, place on a dish and garnish with the remaining spring onion.

WHAT YOU'LL NEED FROM YOUR STORE CUPBOARD
•sesame oil•garlic•salt & pepper•soy sauce

SPECIAL FRIED RICE

5 Ingredients

- 175g/6oz long grain rice
- 2 eggs, beaten
- 1 red bell pepper, finely chopped
- 100g/3½oz cooked ham, diced
- 100g/3½oz frozen peas

Method

1 Bring a pan of water to boil and add in the rice.

2 Cover the pan with a lid and cook for 10 minutes, unless the packet instructions state otherwise.

3 Once cooked, remove the rice from the heat, drain, set to one side and allow to cool.

4 Pre-heat a wok over a high heat and add a splash of vegetable oil.

5 Once the oil is warmed through, crush a fresh clove of garlic into the wok and add the red pepper.

6 Add the cooled rice into the pan, season with salt and pepper, and fry for 5 minutes.

7 Pour in the beaten eggs and stir-fry until the eggs set.

8 Next, add in the ham and peas, stir well, and fry for 4–5 minutes, or until warmed through. To serve, place the rice into a bowl and enjoy hot.

WHAT YOU'LL NEED FROM YOUR STORE CUPBOARD
•vegetable oil•garlic•salt & pepper

CHICKEN FRIED RICE

nom

5 Ingredients

- 150g/5½oz long grain rice
- 1 large egg, beaten
- 1 large chicken breast, finely sliced
- 60g/2½oz frozen peas
- 2 spring onions, thinly sliced

Method

1 Pour 300ml/10floz of water into a saucepan and bring to the boil. Reduce the heat and add in the rice, cover with a lid, and cook for 10-12 minutes, or until cooked through. Remove from the heat, drain and set aside to completely cool.

2 Meanwhile, heat a wok over medium heat and add a in a splash of sesame oil.

3 Add in the egg and cook until scrambled, stirring often with a spatula. Remove the eggs from the pan and place onto a plate.

4 Add in another good splash to the wok and add in the sliced chicken, along with 2 cloves of freshly minced garlic.

5 Seasoning with a small pinch of salt and pepper and stir-fry for 2-3 minutes, or until the chicken is completely sealed and almost cooked through.

6 Next, add the cooked rice, frozen peas, most of the spring onion and scrambled egg.

7 Pour in 2 tablespoons of soy sauce and cook for 3-4 minutes, stirring continuously. Serve straight from the wok and enjoy warm, topped with the remaining spring onion.

WHAT YOU'LL NEED FROM YOUR STORE CUPBOARD
•sesame oil•garlic•salt & pepper•soy sauce

PINEAPPLE AND CASHEW NUT FRIED RICE

nom

5 Ingredients

- 200g/7oz brown jasmine rice
- 1 can of pineapple, juice and chunks
- 2 red bell pepper, de-seeded and thinly sliced
- 2 large eggs, beaten
- 75g/3oz cashew nuts

Method

1 In a large saucepan, combine the rice, pineapple juice and 400ml/14floz of water. Stir thoroughly.

2 Bring the pan to the boil, cover, and then reduce to a simmer, allowing the rice to cook for 25-30 minutes ,or until all the liquid has been absorbed. Once cooked, set the rice aside to cool completely.

3 Place a large wok over a medium-high heat and add in a splash of vegetable oil. Add in the red pepper and 3 minced cloves of garlic, season with salt and pepper, and stir-fry for 2-3 minutes.

4 Add in the pineapple chunks and fry for another minute, then remove the vegetables from the pan and set aside. Add a splash more oil to the pan and pour in the beaten eggs, stirring often with a spatula, and cook until scrambled.

5 Remove the eggs from the pan and place onto a plate.

6 If needed, add a drizzle more oil into the pan before adding in the jasmine rice . Fry for 3 minutes, or until crispy and golden.

7 Lower the heat and add in 2 tablespoons of soy sauce, the vegetables and pineapple, and then the cashew nuts. Cook for another couple of minutes, or until heated through, and serve straight away.

WHAT YOU'LL NEED FROM YOUR STORE CUPBOARD

•vegetable oil•garlic•salt & pepper•soy sauce

CHILLI PRAWN NOODLES

nom

5 Ingredients

- 250g/9oz medium egg noodles
- 300g/11oz beansprouts
- 1 red chilli, finely chopped
- 400g/14oz large prawns, peeled and un-cooked
- 1 handful of sesame seeds

Method

1 Bring a pan of water to the boil and cook the egg noodles according to the packet instructions.

2 Once cooked, rinse with cold water, drain and set to one side.

3 Pre-heat a wok over a high heat and add in a splash of sesame oil.

4 Add in the beansprouts and stir-fry for 2 minutes.

5 Next, add the chilli, along with 3 minced cloves of garlic, and cook for 1 minute, stirring every 10-15 seconds, before adding in the prawns.

6 Stir-fry for 2-3 minutes, or until the prawns just turn pink.

7 Add in 1 tablespoon of brown sugar and 1 tablespoon of soy sauce and fry until all the sugar has dissolved.

8 Place the noodles into the pan along with a drizzle of sesame oil and toss everything together.

9 Once heated through, serve immediately into a bowl and garnish by scattering sesame seeds over the top.

WHAT YOU'LL NEED FROM YOUR STORE CUPBOARD
•sesame oil•garlic•brown sugar•soy sauce

SOY SAUCE PAN-FRIED NOODLES

nom

5 Ingredients

- 225g/8oz thin Hong Kong style egg noodles
- ½ tbsp shaoxing wine
- 2 scallions, julienned
- 200g/7oz beansprouts

Method

1 Bring a pan of water to boil and cook the noodles. Once cooked, rinse in cold water and drain. In a bowl mix 2 tbsp of soy sauce with plenty of salt & pepper. Stir well, then add in ¼ of a teaspoon of sugar and the shaoxing wine. Stir once more and place to one side ready to use shortly.

2 Heat a wok over a high heat and add in a tablespoon of vegetable oil. Add in the noodles and fry for 4 minutes. Flip the noodles over, add another tablespoon of oil around the edge of the pan, and fry for another 3-4 minutes to crisp up the other side.

3 Once crisp, remove the noodles and set them aside. Next, add some more oil to the pan and fry the white parts of the scallion for 20-25 seconds, before returning the noodles to the pan.

4 Toss the noodles, using a spatula to break up any clumps, then add in the soy sauce mixture and toss frequently for a couple of minutes.

5 Once the noodles are evenly covered, mix in the beansprouts and the remaining scallions and fry for a further 2 minutes.

6 When the beansprouts are cooked but still crunchy, serve immediately and enjoy.

WHAT YOU'LL NEED FROM YOUR STORE CUPBOARD
•soy sauce•brown sugar•vegetable oil

BROCCOLI & CHICKEN NOODLES

5 Ingredients

- 1 red chilli, de-seeded and sliced
- 2 chicken breasts, skinless and cut into strips
- 1 small head of broccoli, cut into florets
- 225g/8oz fresh medium egg noodles
- 300g beansprouts

Method

1 Begin by preparing the marinade; stir 3 minced cloves of garlic, the red chilli, 1 tablespoon of soy sauce and 2 tablespoons of tomato puree together in a bowl.

2 Add in the chicken, stirring well and folding the chicken strips into the marinade to evenly coat.

3 Allow the chicken to marinade for 10 – 15 minutes.

4 Bring a saucepan of water to boil and cook the broccoli for 2-3 minutes.

5 Add in the noodles for 3-4 minutes. Rinse, drain and set to one side.

6 Meanwhile, heat a wok over a high heat and add in a splash of vegetable oil.

7 Add the marinated chicken strips, along with any excess marinade, into the pan and stir-fry for 4-5 minutes, until the chicken is cooked through.

8 Add in the broccoli, noodles and beansprouts and leave for a minute to warm through.

9 Then, pour in a splash more sesame oil and a tablespoon of soy sauce, and toss everything together, just before serving.

WHAT YOU'LL NEED FROM YOUR STORE CUPBOARD
•garlic•soy sauce•tomato puree•vegetable oil•sesame oil

HOISIN CHINESE DUCK NOODLES

5 Ingredients

- 2 duck breasts, skin left on
- 5oz/150g dried egg noodles
- 1 tbsp peanut butter
- 1 cucumber, julienned
- 1 spring onion, thinly sliced

Method

1 Preheat the oven to 220C/425F/Gas 7.

2 Take each duck breast and score the skin with a crisscross pattern, then rub in some Chinese five-spice powder and sesame oil.

3 Place the duck on a roasting tray and cook for 15 minutes.

4 Meanwhile, bring a pan of water to the boil and cook the noodles for 5-6 minutes, or longer according to the packet instructions.

5 Drain and rinse the noodles, then toss them in a bowl with a splash of sesame oil.

6 To make a homemade hoisin sauce, add the peanut butter, 2 tablespoons of soy sauce, half a tablespoon of brown sugar, 1 teaspoon rice vinegar, a pinch pepper, 1 teaspoon of sesame oil and 1 crushed garlic clove into a food processor or blender and blitz to a smooth liquid.

7 Once the duck is cooked, slice the breasts and place into a large bowl.

8 Then, add in the noodles, hoisin sauce and cucumber, and toss everything together until there is an even coating. To serve, divide the mixture evenly onto plates and sprinkle over the chopped spring onion.

WHAT YOU'LL NEED FROM YOUR STORE CUPBOARD

•Chinese 5 spice•sesame oil•soy sauce•brown sugar•rice vinegar•black pepper•sesame oil•garlic

MUSHROOM FRIED RICE

5 Ingredients

- 300g/11oz long grain rice
- 2 eggs, beaten
- 1 small onion, finely diced
- 6 medium mushrooms, thinly sliced
- 40g/1½oz peas

Method

1 Bring a pan of water to boil and add in the rice.

2 Cover the pan with a lid and cook for 10-12 minutes, unless the packet instructions state otherwise.

3 Once cooked, remove the rice, drain, set aside, and allow to completely cool.

4 Heat a wok over a medium-high heat and add in a splash of sesame oil.

5 Pour in the eggs and stir with a spatula until scrambled, then remove and set aside.

6 Add some more oil to the pan and stir-fry the onion and mushrooms for 2-3 minutes, until the mushrooms are tender but not over cooked.

7 Crush 1 clove of fresh garlic, add it into the pan and fry for another minute.

8 Next, stir in the peas, cooled rice, 6 tablespoons of soy sauce, a teaspoon of sesame oil, and a pinch of salt and pepper.

9 Toss everything together and heat through for around 4 minutes.

10 Serve straight from the wok.

WHAT YOU'LL NEED FROM YOUR STORE CUPBOARD
•sesame oil•garlic•soy sauce•salt & pepper

SINGAPORE MEI FUN

nom

5 Ingredients

- 1 Chinese sausage (Lop Cheung), diced
- 1 red chilli pepper, deseeded and sliced
- 2 carrots, julienned
- 100g/3½oz Chinese cabbage, shredded
- 225g/8oz fresh rice noodles

Method

1 Pre-heat a wok over a high heat and add in a splash of sesame oil.

2 Once the oil is warmed, add in the sausage and stir-fry for 20-25 seconds.

3 Add in the chilli pepper, carrot and cabbage, and fry for a further minute.

4 Next, sprinkle 2 tablespoons of curry powder evenly over the contents of the pan and stir well.

5 Place the rice noodles into the pan and break up any clumps.

6 Pour in a tablespoon of rice vinegar, a tablespoon of soy sauce and a pinch of salt.

7 Stir the mixture continuously for 3-4 minutes and then serve straight from the wok.

WHAT YOU'LL NEED FROM YOUR STORE CUPBOARD
•sesame oil•curry powder•rice vinegar•soy sauce•salt

NASI GORENG

5 Ingredients

- 300g/11oz long-grain rice
- 4 large eggs, beaten
- 150g/5oz green beans, trimmed and halved
- 2 chicken breasts, skinless and diced
- 1 tsbp kecap manis

Method

1 Bring a pan of water to boil and add in the rice. Cover, reduce and cook for 10-12 minutes unless the packet instructions state otherwise. Once cooked, remove the rice, drain and set aside.

2 Heat a wok on a medium heat with a little oil, and pour in the egg, using a spatula to shape it into an omelette. Cook for a couple of minutes, until the mixture has set, then flip over and repeat on the other side.

3 Once the omelette is cooked, remove and place onto a plate to cool before cutting it into long shreds.

4 Meanwhile, blanch the green beans until tender but not overcooked.

5 Add another splash of oil into the pan and stir-fry the chicken for 5-6 minutes.

6 Stir in 1 tablespoon of tomato puree, kecap manis, the cooled rice and green beans, then fry for 2-3 minutes.

7 Next, add in 2 tablespoons of soy sauce and the shredded omelette. Toss everything together for around a minute, then serve the nasi goreng straight from the wok.

WHAT YOU'LL NEED FROM YOUR STORE CUPBOARD
•vegetable oil•tomato puree•soy sauce

BOILED RICE WITH VEGETABLES

5 Ingredients

- 175g/6oz long grain rice
- 50g/2oz frozen peas
- ½ Chinese cabbage, shredded
- 1 carrot, finely chopped
- 1 red bell pepper, finely diced

Method

1 Bring a medium saucepan, containing enough water to cover the rice, to the boil.

2 Reduce to a simmer, then add in the rice.

3 Cook for 2-3 minutes before adding in the peas and leaving to simmer for a further 8-10 minutes, or until the rice is cooked through.

4 Once cooked, rinse, drain and add to a large bowl.

5 Add the cabbage, carrot and red pepper and toss well.

6 To serve, spoon the rice mixture into each bowl and add some soy sauce to taste.

WHAT YOU'LL NEED FROM YOUR STORE CUPBOARD
- soy sauce

SAVOURY RICE

nom

5 Ingredients

- 4 button mushrooms, chopped
- 1 red bell pepper, sliced
- 175g/6oz long grain rice
- 600ml/1 pint vegetable stock
- 60g/2½oz frozen peas

Method

1 Pre-heat a wok on a medium-high heat and add a splash of vegetable oil.

2 Fry the mushrooms and red peppers for 2 minutes.

3 Stir the rice into the pan and add in the vegetable stock, peas, and 2 tablespoons of curry powder.

4 Allow the mixture to simmer for 15 minutes, until the rice is tender and the liquid is fully absorbed, stirring occasionally.

5 Once cooked, serve immediately whilst still warm.

WHAT YOU'LL NEED FROM YOUR STORE CUPBOARD
•vegetable oil•curry powder

SINGAPORE STYLE FRIED RICE

5 Ingredients

- 200g/7oz long grain rice
- 1 egg, beaten
- 40g/1½oz frozen peas
- 100g/3½oz prawns, peeled and de-veined
- 2 spring onions, thinly sliced

Method

1 Bring a saucepan, containing enough water to cover the rice, to the boil.

2 Reduce the heat and add in the long grain rice. Cover, cook for 10-12 minutes unless the packet instructions state otherwise

3 Once cooked, drain and set to one side, allowing the rice to cool completely.

4 Heat a wok over high heat and add in a splash of sesame oil.

5 Pour in the egg and stir until it scrambles.

6 Next, add in the peas and prawns and stir-fry until the prawns turn pink.

7 Add the boiled rice and spring onions into the wok and fry for 3-4 minutes, breaking up any lumps of rice with a spatula.

8 Season with a pinch of salt and pepper and add 2 tablespoons of soy sauce.

9 Stir-fry for a further 3-4 minutes, then serve in a bowl to enjoy straight away.

WHAT YOU'LL NEED FROM YOUR STORE CUPBOARD
•sesame oil•salt & pepper•soy sauce

PRAWN NOODLE SALAD

nom

5 Ingredients

- 225g/8oz fresh medium egg noodles
- 200g/7oz king prawns, peeled
- ½ large cucumber, sliced into halfmoons
- 100g/3½oz cherry tomatoes, cut into halves
- 4 tbsp sweet chilli sauce

Method

1 Bring a medium saucepan of water to the boil and cook the noodles for 4-5 minutes, unless the packet instructions state otherwise.

2 Rinse the noodles with cold water and drain.

3 Cut the noodles into shorter lengths and place them in a large bowl – you may find it easiest to cut them with scissors.

4 Meanwhile, heat a wok over a high heat.

5 Drizzle in some sesame oil and add 2 minced cloves of garlic, followed by the prawns.

6 Stir-fry for 4-5 minutes, until the prawns have turned pink and are cooked through.

7 Once cooked, add the garlic prawns into the bowl of chopped noodles, along with the cucumber, tomatoes and sweet chilli sauce, and toss together to make sure everything is coated.

8 To serve, place the noodle salad onto plates or into a large serving bowl for everyone to dive into.

WHAT YOU'LL NEED FROM YOUR STORE CUPBOARD
•sesame oil•garlic

nom nom
CHINESE
takeaway kitchen

VEGETABLES

SPICY STARFRUIT SALAD

nom

5 Ingredients

- 2 tbsp honey
- 1 Asian shallot, sliced
- 1 starfruit, thinly sliced
- 100g/3½oz curly morning glory
- 1 red chilli, thinly sliced

Method

1 To make the salad dressing, combine the honey and shallots together in a bowl.

2 Add in a freshly crushed clove of garlic, 2 tablespoons of oyster sauce and some salt and pepper to season. Place the dressing to one side ready to drizzle over the salad later.

3 Add the sliced starfruit, curly morning glory and sliced chilli in a bowl and toss well. To serve, drizzle over the dressing.

WHAT YOU'LL NEED FROM YOUR STORE CUPBOARD
•garlic•oyster sauce•salt & pepper

GREEN TOFU ASIAN SALAD

nom

5 Ingredients

- The juice of 1 fresh lime
- 100g/3½oz mangetout
- 200g/7oz green beans
- ½ head of broccoli, cut into florets
- 200g/7oz silken tofu, diced

Method

1 Place a double-layer steamer over a large pan of water and bring to the boil.

2 Meanwhile, prepare the dressing by crushing one clove of garlic and mixing it with 2 tablespoons of soy sauce and sesame oil, as well as the lime juice.

3 Place the mangetout, green beans and broccoli into the top layer of the steamer and the cubed tofu in the bottom layer.

4 Steam everything for 4-5 minutes, or until the vegetables are just cooked.

5 Toss the vegetables and tofu together and serve immediately with brown rice noodles, or a noodle of your choice.

WHAT YOU'LL NEED FROM YOUR STORE CUPBOARD
•garlic•soy sauce•sesame oil

MIXED VEGETABLE CURRY

nom

5 Ingredients

- 250g/9oz sweet potato, peeled and roughly chopped
- 200g/7oz curry paste
- 200g/7oz cauliflower, cut into florets
- 250g/9oz green beans, trimmed
- 200ml/7floz coconut milk

Method

1 Brush the sweet potato chunks with vegetable oil and cook in a microwave on a medium-high heat for 10 minutes.

2 Add the curry paste to 450ml/15½floz of water, unless the packet instructions state otherwise.

3 Pour into a large pan and bring to the boil.

4 Meanwhile, in another pan of boiling water, blanch the cauliflower for 3-4 minutes, then drain and set aside.

5 When the curry sauce begins to boil, add in the cauliflower, green beans and sweet potato and cook for 5-6 minutes.

6 Next, add in the coconut milk and boil for another couple of minutes.

7 Once cooked, serve on its own, or with some steamed rice.

WHAT YOU'LL NEED FROM YOUR STORE CUPBOARD
- vegetable oil

SWEET AND SOUR MIXED VEGETABLES

nom

5 Ingredients

- 1 tin of pineapple, chunks and juice
- 2 yellow peppers, de-seeded and chopped
- ½ a cauliflower, cut into florets
- 1 head broccoli, cut into florets
- 50g/2oz mangetout

Method

1 To make the sauce, combine the juice from the pineapple, 1 tablespoon of cornflour, a pinch of salt, 3 tablespoons of brown sugar and a splash of rice vinegar, mix thoroughly and set to one side.

2 Pre-heat a wok or large saucepan over a medium-high heat and add in a splash of vegetable oil.

3 Once hot, add in the vegetables and stir-fry for 5-6 minutes until tender.

4 Next, add in the pineapple chunks and stir for 1 minute, or until the sauce thickens.

5 Serve immediately whilst still hot.

WHAT YOU'LL NEED FROM YOUR STORE CUPBOARD
•salt •brown sugar•rice vinegar
•vegetable oil

MUSHROOMS IN HOT GARLIC SAUCE

nom

5 Ingredients

- 1 small onion, peeled and chopped
- 1 red chilli, finely sliced
- 200g/7oz button mushrooms, washed
- 1 red bell pepper, de-seeded and chopped
- 1 spring onion, finely sliced

Method

1 To make the sauce, whisk together 2 tablespoons of cornflour and 12 tablespoons of water in a bowl. Add in 1 teaspoon of salt, 1 tablespoon of soy sauce, 1 tablespoon of brown sugar and 4 tablespoons of rice vinegar and whisk well again.

2 The sauce should achieve a syrup-like consistency; add in more water or flour if required.

3 Meanwhile, pre-heat a wok over high heat and add in a splash of sesame oil.

4 Add in 2 crushed garlic cloves , onion and red chilli, and fry until the garlic softens. Then, add in the mushrooms and bell pepper and stir-fry for 2 minutes.

5 Pour in a splash of water, along with the sauce mixture, and bring to a boil, stirring continuously.

6 Once the sauce thickens, add in the spring onion and simmer for 1 minute.

7 Remove from the heat and serve.

WHAT YOU'LL NEED FROM YOUR STORE CUPBOARD
•salt•soy sauce•brown sugar•rice vinegar•garlic

56

VEGETABLE FRIED RICE

nom

5 Ingredients

- 150g/5oz brown rice
- 1 small red onion, peeled and chopped
- 3 spring onions, thinly sliced
- 100g/3½oz garden peas, frozen or fresh
- A small handful of cashew nuts, crushed

Method

1 Over a high heat, bring a pan of water to the boil.

2 Add in the rice, cover and allow to simmer for around 20 minutes, unless the packet instructions state otherwise.

3 Meanwhile, pre-heat a wok on a medium heat. Add in a drizzle of sesame oil.

4 Once hot, add in one freshly crushed garlic clove and the chopped onion and cook for 2-3 minutes, stirring often.

5 Once cooked, drain the rice, add it into the frying pan and increase the temperature to a medium-high heat.

6 Add in the spring onions along with 3 tablespoons of soy sauce and stir-fry for 1 minute. Next, add in the peas and allow to fry for a further minute.

7 Remove from the heat, stir in a tablespoon of sesame oil and mix thoroughly.

8 Serve immediately with a scattering of crushed cashew nuts.

WHAT YOU'LL NEED FROM YOUR STORE CUPBOARD
•sesame oil•garlic•soy sauce•sesame oil

MIXED PEPPERS IN BLACK BEAN SAUCE

nom

5 Ingredients

- 50g/2oz fermented black beans
- 2 inches of fresh ginger, peeled and grated
- 2 green peppers, de-seeded and chopped
- A handful of peanuts, chopped
- 175ml/6floz vegetable broth

Method

1 Begin by preparing the black bean sauce. In a food processor add the black beans, half of the ginger and 3 cloves of crushed fresh garlic. Blend together until a reasonably smooth mixture is achieved.

2 Warm a wok on a medium heat and add in a drizzle of vegetable oil. Add in the chopped peppers and cook for 2-3 minutes, stirring occasionally, until they begin to soften.

3 Add in the remaining ginger and peanuts, and cook for a further minute. Pour in the black bean mixture along with 2 tablespoons of brown sugar, the vegetable broth, a tablespoon of rice vinegar and soy sauce. Whisk the ingredients together and allow to simmer for around 7-10 minutes.

4 Meanwhile, in a bowl, whisk ¼ cup cold water with 1 tablespoon of cornflour. Add to the pan and stir thoroughly just before you remove the pan from the heat.

5 Pre-heat a wok over a medium-high heat and add a splash of sesame oil. Add in the ginger and peppers and stir-fry for 3-4 minutes, until tender but not overcooked. Stir in the black bean sauce and continue heating until warmed through.

WHAT YOU'LL NEED FROM YOUR STORE CUPBOARD
•garlic•vegetable oil•brown sugar•rice vinegar•soy sauce•sesame oil

MUSHROOM CHOP SUEY

5 Ingredients

- 1 onion, peeled and finely chopped
- 2 carrots, peeled and sliced
- 450g/1lb button mushrooms, chopped
- 1 celery, chopped
- 300g/11oz fresh beansprouts

Method

1 Pre-heat a wok or frying pan on medium-high heat and add in a splash of sesame oil.

2 Add in the onion, carrot and 2 minced cloves of garlic, and stir-fry for 3-4 minutes.

3 Next, add in the mushrooms, celery and beansprouts.

4 Place a lid on the pan and fry for 5-6 minutes, until the vegetables are tender, stirring every few minutes.

5 Meanwhile, in a bowl, combine 2 teaspoons of cornflour, 2 tablespoons of water, 2 tablespoons of soy sauce, 1 tablespoon of rice vinegar and a pinch of brown sugar.

6 Whisk until the cornflour has completely dissolved.

7 Pour the sauce into the wok and stir, ensuring that the vegetables are thoroughly coated. Allow to cook for a further 4-5 minutes, or until the sauce thickens.

WHAT YOU'LL NEED FROM YOUR STORE CUPBOARD
•sesame oil•garlic•soy sauce•rice vinegar•brown sugar

MUSHROOM FOO YOUNG

nom

5 Ingredients

- 8 mushrooms, chopped
- 125g/4oz beansprouts
- 6 eggs
- 40g/1½oz frozen peas
- 2 spring onions, thinly sliced

Method

1 Pre-heat a wok over a high heat and add in a splash of vegetable oil. Add the chopped mushrooms and stir-fry for 2 minutes. Add in the beansprouts and fry for a further minute.

2 Crack the eggs into a bowl, whisk well and place to one side.

3 Add the peas into the wok and cook for 3-4 minutes. Remove from the heat and pour the contents of the pan into the bowl containing the beaten eggs.

4 Season the mixture with a good pinch of salt and black pepper. Return the wok to the heat and add in another splash of oil. Give the egg and vegetables a good stir, before pouring the mixture back into the pan.

5 Use a spatula to scramble the mixture and then leave to cook.

6 Flip with a spatula, then allow it to cook for another minute until golden.

7 Serve and garnish with the finely sliced spring onion.

WHAT YOU'LL NEED FROM YOUR STORE CUPBOARD
•vegetable oil•salt & pepper

TOFU FOO YUNG

nom

5 Ingredients

- 150g/5oz snow peas
- 175g/6oz mushrooms, sliced
- 6 spring onions, sliced
- 200g/7oz beansprouts
- 800g/1¾ lb tofu

Method

1 Pre-heat the oven to 170C/325F/Gas 3.

2 Meanwhile, place a wok on a medium-high heat and add in a splash of sesame oil to warm. Add in the snow peas, mushrooms and spring onions, and stir-fry for 4-5 minutes.

3 Next, add in the beansprouts and fry for a further minute, stirring often.

4 Meanwhile, in a food processor add half of the tofu and 2 tablespoons of soy sauce and blitz until smooth.

5 Transfer the sauce into a large bowl and mix in the rest of the tofu by hand, along with 2 teaspoons of baking powder and 75g/3oz of plain flour.

6 Remove the vegetables from the heat and add them into the bowl, mixing well.

7 To make each omelette, spoon 4 tablespoons of the tofu mixture onto baking paper and flatten gently to a thickness of ½ an inch.

8 Repeat until you have used all of the mixture, then bake in the oven for 30 minutes.

9 Turn over each one and cook for a further 12 minutes, or until cooked through, and then serve straight away.

WHAT YOU'LL NEED FROM YOUR STORE CUPBOARD

•sesame oil•plain flour

SWEET CHILLI TOFU

5 Ingredients

- 2 red bell peppers, de-seeded and finely sliced
- 6 spring onions, finely sliced
- 4 tbsp sweet chilli sauce
- 400g/14oz firm tofu, diced into small chunks
- 1 tin of pineapple, juice and chunks

Method

1 Pre-heat a wok over a medium-high heat.

2 Add in a splash of vegetable oil and stir-fry the red peppers and half of the spring onion for 2-3 minutes.

3 Pour in the sweet chilli sauce, along with 2 tablespoons of soy sauce and 3 tablespoons of the pineapple juice, and mix well.

4 Add in the tofu and cook until the sauce begins to thicken to a syrup-like consistency.

5 Mix in the pineapple chunks and cook for a couple of minutes until warmed through.

6 Serve immediately garnished with the remaining spring onion.

WHAT YOU'LL NEED FROM YOUR STORE CUPBOARD
•vegetable oil•soy sauce

BAMBOO SHOOTS & MIXED VEGETABLES CHINESE STYLE

5 Ingredients

- 50g/2oz Chinese mushrooms
- 1 red bell pepper, de-seeded and finely sliced
- 1 carrot, peeled and cut into strips
- 75g/3oz beansprouts
- 250g/9oz bamboo shoots

Method

1 Pre-heat a wok over medium-high high and add in a good splash of vegetable oil.

2 Add all the vegetables, beansprouts and bamboo shoots to the wok and stir-fry for 1 minute.

3 Then, pour in 3 tablespoons of soy sauce, 1 tablespoon of rice vinegar, 1 tablespoon of water and half a teaspoon of brown sugar.

4 Mix well and allow the mixture to simmer for 2 minutes.

5 Stir in 2 teaspoons of cornflour to thicken the sauce, stirring frequently until all the cornflour dissolves.

6 Serve straight from the wok.

WHAT YOU'LL NEED FROM YOUR STORE CUPBOARD
•soy sauce•rice vinegar•brown sugar

LEMON AND GARLIC VEG WITH BAMBOO SHOOTS

5 Ingredients

- 4 tbsp of freshly squeezed lemon juice
- 100g/3½oz mangetout
- 100g/3½oz asparagus, trimmed and chopped
- 150g/5oz bamboo shoots
- 225g/8oz tin of water chestnuts, drained

Method

1 In a large bowl, whisk together 4 freshly minced cloves of garlic, 4 tablespoons of lemon juice, 4 tablespoons of water, 2 tablespoons of soy sauce and 2 teaspoons of cornflour, and place to one side.

2 Pre-heat a wok over high heat and add in a splash of sesame oil.

3 Add in all the vegetables, bamboo shoots and water chestnuts, and stir-fry for 1-2 minutes.

4 Then, pour in the lemon and garlic sauce and stir-fry for around 5 minutes, or until the vegetables are tender but not overcooked, and the sauce thickens to a syrup-like consistency.

5 If required, add in a little more flour or water in order to achieve the syrup-like consistency. Season to taste with salt and black pepper just before serving.

WHAT YOU'LL NEED FROM YOUR STORE CUPBOARD
•garlic•soy sauce•sesame oil•salt & pepper

MIXED VEGETABLES IN REAL OYSTER SAUCE

5 Ingredients

- 75g/3oz fresh oysters, cooked
- 2 peppers, de-seeded and sliced
- 1 head broccoli, cut into small florets
- ½ a cauliflower, cut into small florets
- 40g/1½oz Chinese mushrooms, chopped

Method

1 Drain the oysters, keep the liquid and put aside. In a food processor, blend the oysters until finely chopped, then transfer into a small saucepan over medium-high heat. Add in the retained liquid and bring to the boil.

2 Reduce the heat once the water is boiling, then cover and allow to simmer for 10-12 minutes. Remove from the heat and add in a pinch of salt.

3 Allow the sauce to cool completely, then drain the mixture through a fine sieve into a measuring jug.

4 Measure the sauce and add around a quarter of the volume in soy sauce, mixing them together in a saucepan. Bring the pan to the boil, then allow to simmer for around 10 minutes.

5 Meanwhile, preheat a wok or saucepan to a medium-high heat and add some vegetable oil. Once hot, add in the peppers, broccoli and cauliflower, and stir-fry until tender for 5-6 minutes.

6 Next, add in the mushrooms and fry for a further 1-2 minutes. Pour in the oyster sauce and allow the mixture to simmer for 1 minute to thicken slightly. Serve immediately whilst still hot.

WHAT YOU'LL NEED FROM YOUR STORE CUPBOARD
•salt•soy sauce•vegetable oil

MUSHROOMS WITH BAMBOO SHOOTS IN GARLIC SAUCE

5 Ingredients

- 100g/3½oz button mushrooms, chopped
- 50g/2oz white onion, roughly chopped
- 100g/3½oz mangetout
- 150g/5oz bamboo shoots
- 225g/8oz tinned water chestnuts, drained

Method

1 Begin by preparing the garlic sauce; crush 4 fresh cloves of garlic into a mixing bowl, along with 4 tablespoons of water and 2 tablespoons of soy sauce.

2 Sieve in 2 teaspoons of cornflour and whisk the mixture well until completely smooth. Place to one side, ready to use shortly.

3 Pre-heat a wok over a high heat and add in a splash of sesame oil.

4 Add in all the vegetables, bamboo shoots and water chestnuts, and stir-fry for 1-2 minutes. Then, pour in the prepared garlic sauce and stir-fry for a further 4-5 minutes, or until the vegetables are tender but not overcooked, and the sauce thickens to a syrup-like consistency.

5 Season to taste with salt and black pepper just before serving.

WHAT YOU'LL NEED FROM YOUR STORE CUPBOARD
•garlic•soy sauce•sesame oil

MEAT/POULTRY/SEAFOOD

CHICKEN CHOP SUEY

5 Ingredients

- 450g/1lb chicken breast, sliced
- 1 onion, peeled and finely chopped
- 50g/2oz green beans, chopped
- 300g/11oz fresh beansprouts
- 2 carrots, peeled and roughly grated

Method

1 Pre-heat a wok or frying pan over a medium-high heat and add in a splash of sesame oil.

2 Add in the sliced chicken and stir-fry for 3-4 minutes, sealing the chicken and stirring well. Add in the chopped onion, green beans and 2 minced cloves of garlic, and stir-fry for a further 3-4 minutes.

3 Next, add in the beansprouts, place a lid on the pan and allow the mixture to cook for a further 3-4 minutes, until the vegetables are tender, stirring every few minutes.

4 Meanwhile, in a bowl, combine 2 teaspoons of cornflour, 2 tablespoons of water, 2 tablespoons of soy sauce, 1 tablespoon of rice vinegar and a pinch of sugar.

5 Whisk until the cornflour has completely dissolved.

6 Pour the sauce into the wok and stir, ensuring that the vegetables are thoroughly coated. Allow to cook for a further 3-4 minutes, or until the sauce thickens.

7 Add in the grated carrot, stir and cook for a final 1-2 minutes.

8 Remove from the heat and serve.

WHAT YOU'LL NEED FROM YOUR STORE CUPBOARD
•sesame oil•garlic•soy sauce
•rice vinegar•brown sugar

CHICKEN IN SWEET AND SOUR SAUCE

5 Ingredients

- 400g/14oz chicken breast, finely chopped
- 50g/2oz onion, roughly chopped
- 75g/3oz broccoli florets
- 75g/3oz yellow pepper, de-seeded and chopped
- 1 tin of pineapple

Method

1 Begin by preparing the base for the sweet and sour sauce by adding 1 tablespoon of cornflour and 1 tablespoon of water into a bowl and whisking them together well. Put aside.

2 Place a wok on a medium heat. Drizzle in a good splash of vegetable oil and, once hot, add in the chicken and cook for 3-4 minutes, until sealed and mostly cooked through.

3 Next, add in the chopped onion, pepper and broccoli, and cook for a further 3-4 minutes, or until the vegetables begin to soften.

4 Drain the pineapple and retain the juice - you will need this later. Chop the pineapple into chunks and, along with the saved juice, add into the wok and stir well.

5 Add in 75ml/3floz of rice vinegar, 75g/3oz of brown sugar, 1 tablespoon of soy sauce and 3 tablespoons of tomato ketchup, stir well, and bring to a boil.

6 Add in the cornflour mixture and stir well once more.

7 Cook for 2-3 minutes, stirring occasionally, and serve straight from the wok.

WHAT YOU'LL NEED FROM YOUR STORE CUPBOARD
•vegetable oil•rice vinegar•soy sauce•tomato ketchup

CHINESE-STYLE CHICKEN BURGER

5 Ingredients

- 1 thick slice of bread, crusts removed
- 4 spring onions, chopped
- 450g/1lb chicken breasts, chopped
- 1 red chilli, deseeded and finely chopped
- 1 sprig of fresh coriander, finely chopped

Method

1 Pre-heat the oven to 200C/400F/Gas 6.

2 First, add the bread, spring onion, and 2 cloves of garlic into a food processor and blitz.

3 Next, add the chicken to the food processor, along with the red chilli and coriander.

4 Blitz the mixture to a mince ,but be careful not to overdo it.

5 Combine a couple of drops of soy sauce with the mixture, then gently mould into four flattened burger shapes by hand.

6 Place a frying pan on medium heat and pour in a drizzle of sesame oil.

7 Once hot, fry the burger for around 2 minutes on each side, to gain colour and seal.

8 Finish cooking the burgers in the oven for 10-12 minutes, or until cooked through.

9 Once cooked, these burgers are great served inside a toasted bun with a drizzle of chilli sauce and rocket.

WHAT YOU'LL NEED FROM YOUR STORE CUPBOARD
•garlic•soy sauce•sesame oil

TERIYAKI BEEF

nom

5 Ingredients

- 400g/14oz frying steak, thinly sliced
- 1 spring onion, finely sliced
- 1 small red chilli, de-seeded and finely sliced
- 1 inch piece of fresh ginger, grated
- 2 tbsp runny honey

Method

1 Place a small pan over medium-high heat and add in a drizzle of sesame oil.

2 Add the steak slices and cook for 2-3 minutes, stirring regularly so the beef is evenly sealed.

3 Add in the spring onion and red chilli, and stir-fry for a further minute.

4 Next, add 120ml/4floz of soy sauce, a splash of sesame oil, the ginger and honey, 2 tablespoons of rice vinegar, 2 tablespoons of brown sugar and 2 crushed cloves of garlic into the pan.

5 Stir well and allow to simmer for 2-3 minutes.

6 In a bowl, whisk 1 tablespoon of cornflour and 4 tablespoons of water, then add to the pan, stirring well.

7 Reduce the heat and allow the teriyaki beef to simmer for 5-7 minutes, or until the sauce begins to thicken.

8 Remove from the heat and serve straight away.

WHAT YOU'LL NEED FROM YOUR STORE CUPBOARD

•sesame oil•soy sauce•rice vinegar•brown sugar•garlic

SWEET AND SOUR SQUID

nom

5 Ingredients

- 250g/9oz squid tentacles, cleaned
- ½ red chilli, de-seeded and chopped
- 3 tomatoes, cut into wedges
- 200g/7oz tinned pineapple, chunks and juice
- ½ courgette, ends removed and diced

Method

1 Chop up the squid to create rings that are roughly half a centimetre in width, keeping the tentacles whole.

2 In a mortar and pestle add a crushed clove of fresh garlic, 2 teaspoons of brown sugar and the chopped chilli, and crush to a paste.

3 Add in a dash of fish sauce and blend with a spoon.

4 Meanwhile, place a wok on a high heat and add in a drop of sesame oil.

5 Once hot, stir-fry the tomatoes for 1 minute.

6 Then, add in the tinned pineapple, including the juice, as well as the chopped courgette.

7 Stir well and cook for 3-4 minutes.

8 Once cooked, serve immediately.

WHAT YOU'LL NEED FROM YOUR STORE CUPBOARD
•brown sugar•fish sauce•sesame oil

PORK AND BAMBOO SHOOTS CHINESE STYLE

nom

5 Ingredients

- 350g/12oz pork steak, finely sliced
- 50g/2oz onion, peeled and chopped
- 250g/9oz bamboo shoots
- 1 green bell pepper, de-seeded and finely sliced
- 1 carrot, peeled and cut into strips

Method

1 Pre-heat a wok over medium-high high and add in a good splash of vegetable oil.

2 Add the sliced pork and cook for 4-5 minutes, stirring regularly to evenly seal..

3 Once the pork is almost cooked through, add in the onion, bamboo shoots, pepper and carrot, and stir-fry for 1 minute.

4 Next, pour in 3 tablespoons of soy sauce, 1 tablespoon of rice vinegar, 1 tablespoon of water and half a teaspoon of brown sugar.

5 Mix thoroughly and allow to simmer for 2-3 minutes.

6 Sieve in 2 teaspoons of cornflour to thicken the sauce, stirring frequently until all the cornflour dissolves, then serve straight from the wok.

WHAT YOU'LL NEED FROM YOUR STORE CUPBOARD
•vegetable oil•soy sauce•brown sugar

GRIDDLED TUNA CHUNKS

5 Ingredients

- 2 tuna steaks, skinned and boned
- 1 sprig of fresh coriander, finely chopped
- 1 sprig of dill, finely chopped
- The juice of 1 lemon

Method

1 Chop the tuna steaks roughly into large chunks and place to one side.

2 In a bowl, add in 4 tablespoons of sesame oil and finely chopped herbs.

3 Mix well and squeeze in the juice of 1 lemon.

4 Add in a freshly crushed clove of garlic and season with salt and black pepper.

5 Mix well, then roll the tuna chunks in the mixture, ensuring that they are thoroughly coated.

6 Meanwhile, pre-heat the griddle to a high heat.

7 Once hot, add in the coated tuna chunks.

8 Allow the fish to cook for around 2 minutes on each side, with the tuna being seared on the outside and pink in the middle.

9 Once cooked, serve immediately with a wedge of lemon.

WHAT YOU'LL NEED FROM YOUR STORE CUPBOARD
•sesame oil•garlic•salt & pepper

KUNG PO CHICKEN

nom

5 Ingredients

- 3 tbsp shaoxing wine
- 600g/1lb 5oz skinless chicken breast, diced
- ½ green bell pepper, de-seeded and chopped
- ½ red bell pepper, de-seeded and chopped
- 4 spring onions, finely sliced

Method

1 Make the marinade: combine 1 tablespoon of shaoxing wine with 2 teaspoons of baking soda and 1 tablespoon of soy sauce. Add to the chicken, ensuring it is fully coated, then cover and leave to marinate for 10-15 minutes.

2 Meanwhile, prepare the sauce by mixing 4 tablespoons of soy sauce, 2 teaspoons of hoisin sauce, 2 tablespoons of shaoxing wine, 2 tablespoons of brown sugar and 120ml/4floz of water. Whisk the mixture until the brown sugar dissolves, then place to one side.

3 Pre-heat a wok on a high heat and add a little sesame oil. Add the chicken and fry for 4–5 minutes, or until the chicken is cooked. Remove the chicken and set aside.

4 Into the same pan, add in another splash of sesame oil and then stir in 4 crushed cloves of garlic and the sliced peppers, then stir-fry for a further minute. Next, pour in the sauce prepared earlier.

5 Once it begins to thicken, return the chicken to the pan and mix continuously for 2 minutes. Stir in the spring onions and continue to cook for a further 2-3 minutes, then serve straight from the pan.

WHAT YOU'LL NEED FROM YOUR STORE CUPBOARD
•baking soda•soy sauce•hoisin sauce•brown sugar•sesame oil•garlic

PLAIN CHINESE CHICKEN BALLS

nom

·····5 Ingredients·····

- 2 skinless chicken breasts, diced
- 1 tsp baking powder

Method

1 In a bowl, add 100g/4oz plain flour, a teaspoon of baking powder and a pinch of salt, and mix well with 120ml/4floz cold water to get a cream-like consistency.

2 If the batter goes too runny, you can always sieve in a little more flour to thicken.

3 Allow the batter to sit for around 20 minutes.

4 Spoon 4 tablespoons of cornflour into a bowl.

5 Dip the chicken chunks into the cornflour and then into the batter, ensuring they are evenly covered, and set them to one side.

6 Pre-heat a saucepan, or deep fat fryer, containing enough vegetable oil to submerge the balls.

7 In batches, add the battered chicken to the hot oil and fry for 4–6 minutes, until they go a golden brown colour.

8 Remove the balls with a slotted spoon and place on kitchen paper to remove excess oil, dabbing the balls all over.

WHAT YOU'LL NEED FROM YOUR STORE CUPBOARD
•plain flour•baking powder•salt•cornflour•vegetable oil

SWEET AND SOUR CHICKEN BALLS

5 Ingredients

- 50g/2oz onion, roughly chopped
- 75g/3oz red pepper, de-seeded and chopped
- 75g/3oz yellow pepper, de-seeded and chopped
- 1 tin of pineapple
- Plain Chinese Chicken Balls for 4 people, cooked

Method

1 First, prepare the sauce by sieving 1 tablespoon of cornflour into a small bowl, and pouring in 1 tablespoon of water. Whisk together well and set to one side.

2 Place a wok on a medium heat. Drizzle in a little sesame oil and, once hot, add in the chopped onion and peppers. Cook for 3-4 minutes, or until the vegetables begin to soften.

3 Open the tin of pineapple, drain it but keep the juice. Chop into chunks and add to the wok along with 75ml/2½floz of rice vinegar, 75g/3oz of brown sugar, 1 tablespoon of soy sauce, 3 tablespoons of tomato ketchup and the juice, and bring to a boil. Add in the cornflour mixture and combine well.

4 Cook for 2 minutes, stirring occasionally, until the sauce thickens.

5 If freshly cooked, add the chicken balls into the wok and stir into the sauce for 1-2 minutes. If chilled, add the chicken balls into the wok, but reduce the heat, and cook for 4-5 minutes, or until completely warmed through, stirring occasionally. Remove from the heat and serve.

WHAT YOU'LL NEED FROM YOUR STORE CUPBOARD

•cornflour•sesame oil•rice vinegar•soy sauce•tomato ketchup

BEEF IN REAL OYSTER SAUCE

5 Ingredients

- 75g/3oz oysters, cooked
- 200g/7oz frying steak, chopped
- 200g/7oz tenderstem broccoli
- 1 medium onion, sliced

Method

1 Begin by draining the oysters - keep the liquid and place to one side. In a food processor blend the oysters until finely chopped, then transfer into a small saucepan over medium-high heat. Add in the retained liquid and bring to the boil.

2 Reduce the heat once the water is boiling, then cover and allow to simmer for 10 to 12 minutes. Remove from the heat and add in a pinch of salt. Allow the sauce to cool, then drain the mixture through a fine sieve into a measuring jug.

3 Measure the sauce and add around a quarter of the volume in soy sauce, mixing them together in a saucepan. Bring the pan to boil and then allow to simmer for around 10 minutes.

4 Preheat a wok and add a little vegetable oil. Add the beef and stir-fry for 2-3 minutes, then set aside. Add in the onion and a crushed clove of garlic, and cook for one minute. Pour in 120ml/4floz of water and the prepared oyster sauce and simmer until the sauce has a thick, sticky consistency.

5 Next, stir in the beef and any juices from the plate. Once cooked through, serve straight away.

WHAT YOU'LL NEED FROM YOUR STORE CUPBOARD
•soy sauce•vegetable oil•garlic

SERVES 4

BEEF CHOP SUEY

5 Ingredients

- 450g/1lb frying steak, cut into strips
- 1 onion, peeled and finely chopped
- 2 carrots, peeled and chopped
- 50g/2oz broccoli, chopped into florets
- 300g/11oz fresh beansprouts

Method

1 Pre-heat a wok or frying pan over a medium-high heat and add in a splash of sesame oil.

2 Add in the sliced frying steak fry for 1-2 minutes, stirring well to seal the beef evenly.

3 Add in the chopped onion, carrots and broccoli, along with 2 minced cloves of garlic, and stir-fry for 3-4 minutes.

4 Next, add in the beansprouts and place a lid on the pan to allow the mixture to cook for a further 3-4 minutes, until the vegetables are tender, stirring every so often.

5 Meanwhile, in a bowl, combine 2 teaspoons of cornflour, 2 tablespoons of water, 2 tablespoons of soy sauce, 1 tablespoon of rice vinegar and a pinch of brown sugar.

6 Whisk until the cornflour has completely dissolved.

7 Pour the sauce into the wok and stir, ensuring that the vegetables are thoroughly coated. Allow to cook for a further 3-4 minutes, or until the sauce thickens.

8 Remove from the heat and serve.

WHAT YOU'LL NEED FROM YOUR STORE CUPBOARD
•sesame oil•garlic•cornflour•soy sauce•rice vinegar•brown sugar

KING PRAWNS WITH GINGER AND SPRING ONION

5 Ingredients

- 1 sprig of coriander, leaves and stalks separated
- 200g/7oz king prawns, peeled

- 1 small knob of ginger, grated
- 6 spring onions, finely sliced
- 100g/3½oz beansprouts

Method

1 Add the coriander stalks, 1 tablespoon of brown sugar and 4 tablespoons of fish sauce to a food processor and blitz together.

2 Place the prawns in a bowl and pour the sauce all over them.

3 Heat a wok on a high heat and add in a splash of sesame oil.

4 Once hot, add in the ginger, spring onions and beansprouts, and stir-fry for 1-2 minutes, or until the beansprouts begin to wilt.

5 Pour in 1 tablespoon of soy sauce and a pinch of black pepper, stir for 1 minute, then place the contents onto a serving dish.

6 Pour a little more sesame oil into the wok and add in the prawns.

7 Stir-fry the prawns, without the juices, for around 2-3 minutes, or until they turn pink, and then add the marinade into the pan.

8 Once heated through thoroughly, pour over the vegetables and garnish with a sprinkling of chopped coriander leaves.

WHAT YOU'LL NEED FROM YOUR STORE CUPBOARD

•sesame oil•brown sugar•fish sauce•black pepper

KING PRAWNS IN REAL OYSTER SAUCE

SERVES 2

nom

5 Ingredients

- 75g/3oz oysters, cooked
- 200g/7oz king prawns, de-shelled and de-veined
- 150g/5oz broccoli florets
- 60g/2½oz bamboo shoots
- 1 medium onion, sliced

Method

1 Drain the cooked oysters and remove them from the shells, but do not dispose of the liquid. Place the oysters in a food processor and blend until smooth. Add the smooth oysters to a saucepan, on a medium-high heat, along with the liquid and bring to the boil. Reduce the heat once the water is boiling, then cover and allow to simmer for 10-12 minutes. Remove from the heat and add in a pinch of salt.

2 Allow the sauce to cool completely, then drain the mixture through a fine sieve into a measuring jug. Measure the sauce and add around a quarter of the volume in soy sauce, mixing together in a saucepan. Bring the pan to boil again and allow to simmer for 8-10 minutes.

3 Place a wok on a high heat and add in a good splash of vegetable oil. Add the king prawns to the pan and stir-fry for 2-3 minutes, or until they start to turn pink. Add a splash of water to the pan and add in the broccoli florets, bamboo shoots and onion, as well as 1 freshly minced clove of garlic, and stir-fry for a further 3-4 minutes, or until the vegetables are just cooked. Next, pour in 120ml/4floz of water and the prepared oyster sauce.

4 Allow the mixture to simmer until the sauce has a thick, sticky consistency. Once completely warmed through, serve immediately.

WHAT YOU'LL NEED FROM YOUR STORE CUPBOARD

•salt•soy sauce•vegetable oil•garlic

SMOKED SHREDDED CHICKEN

SERVES 4

5 Ingredients

- 1 tsp smoked salt
- 1 egg
- 4 skinless chicken breasts, finely sliced
- 3 spring onions, finely sliced
- ½ red chilli, de-seeded and finely sliced

Method

1 In a dish, add enough flour to coat the sliced chicken and season with 1 teaspoon black pepper and the smoked salt.

2 In another bowl, whisk together the egg and 2 tablespoons of hoisin sauce, then stir in the chicken.

3 Pre-heat a saucepan of boiling oil, enough to submerge the chicken pieces, or warm up a deep fat fryer.

4 In small batches, transfer the chicken to the flour mix, ensuring an even coating, and then place them into the hot oil until they have a golden colour.

5 Meanwhile, preheat a frying pan with a little oil.

6 Remove the chicken from the fryer using a slotted spoon and fry in the pan for a few minutes to make the chicken crispy.

7 Mix in a minced clove of garlic, the spring onions and red chilli, and fry for a further 2 minutes, stirring often. To serve, put into a dish and enjoy straight away.

WHAT YOU'LL NEED FROM YOUR STORE CUPBOARD

•plain flour•salt & pepper•hoisin sauce•vegetable oil•garlic

SERVES 4

KUNG PO PRAWNS

5 Ingredients

- 400g/14oz king prawns, peeled
- 75g/3oz peanuts, unsalted
- 450g/1lb water chestnuts, drained
- 1 inch piece of fresh ginger, grated
- 4 spring onions, thinly sliced

Method

1 Add 1 teaspoon of cornflour and 1 tablespoon of soy sauce into a bowl and mix well.

2 Add in the prawns, stirring them into the mixture to ensure they are evenly coated. Leave to marinade for 10-15 minutes.

3 Meanwhile, make a sauce by mixing together 1 tablespoon of soy sauce, 1 heaped tablespoon of tomato puree, 1 teaspoon of brown sugar, 2 tablespoons of rice vinegar and 2 tablespoons of water. Stir well and place to one side.

4 Pre-heat a wok over a high heat and add a splash of sesame oil. Add in the prawns and fry until golden, then remove from the pan and set aside.

5 In the same pan, add a little more sesame oil and stir-fry the peanuts and water chestnuts for 2 minutes.

6 Then, add in the ginger and spring onions, and fry for another minute.

7 Pour in the sauce and prawns and allow to simmer for 2-3 minutes, until the sauce begins to thicken.

8 Serve straight from the wok.

WHAT YOU'LL NEED FROM YOUR STORE CUPBOARD

•cornflour•soy sauce•tomato puree•brown sugar•rice vinegar•sesame oil

SERVES 4

SWEET AND SOUR PORK HONG KONG STYLE

5 Ingredients

- 450g/1lb pork loin, cut into 1-inch cubes
- 150g/5oz potato starch
- 1 egg
- 4 slices of tinned pineapple, chopped
- 2 cayenne peppers, sliced

Method

1 In a bowl, whisk 2 teaspoons of soy sauce, 1 teaspoon of sesame oil, 1 tablespoon of brown sugar, 2 teaspoons of potato starch and a pinch of pepper. Add the pork and rest for 15 minutes.

2 Meanwhile, make the sauce by whisking 2 tablespoons of rice vinegar, 250ml/8½floz of water, 50g/2oz of brown sugar, a pinch of salt, 2 teaspoons of potato starch and 3 tablespoons of tomato ketchup together in a bowl, then place to one side.

3 Crack the egg into a bowl and whisk. Dip the pork into the egg, then into the other starch mixture. Ensure the pieces are evenly coated in each mixture. Pre-heat a saucepan over medium-high heat and add enough sesame oil to submerge the pork in. Fry the pork in hot oil for 4-5 minutes, until

crispy and light brown. Remove from the oil using a slotted spoon and place on kitchen paper to remove excess oil, dabbing all over.

4 Pre-heat a wok over medium heat and add a splash of sesame oil. Fry the pineapple, cayenne pepper and 2 crushed cloves of garlic for 5 minutes. Pour in the sauce and cook until it starts to thicken. Add the pork and mix well. Remove from heat and serve.

WHAT YOU'LL NEED FROM YOUR STORE CUPBOARD
•soy sauce•sesame oil•brown sugar•salt & pepper•rice vinegar•tomato ketchup•garlic

84

CRISPY SHREDDED BEEF

nom

5 Ingredients

- 400g/14oz minute steak, sliced into thin strips
- 1 red bell pepper, de-seeded and thinly sliced
- 1 red chilli, thinly sliced
- 5 spring onions, sliced
- 1 inch piece of ginger, grated

Method

1 Place the strips of steak into a bowl and mix with 2 teaspoons of Chinese five-spice powder and 3 tablespoons of cornflour. Heat a wok over high heat and add in a good splash of vegetable oil. Add in the steak and stir-fry until crisp and golden.

2 Remove the steak and drain using some kitchen towel.

3 Add a little more oil to the pan, then add in the red pepper, half of the sliced chilli, half of the spring onion, 2 minced cloves of garlic, and the ginger.

4 Stir-fry the vegetables for 3-4 minutes, or until they start to soften, stirring often.

5 Meanwhile, add 4 tablespoons of rice vinegar into a bowl, along with 2 tablespoons of tomato ketchup, 2 tablespoons of soy sauce and 3 tablespoons of water.

6 Mix very well until completely blended, then pour this mixture into the pan over the vegetables and allow to simmer for 2 minutes.

7 Add the beef back into the pan and toss well to ensure everything mixes well.

8 Immediately serve onto a dish and scatter with the remaining spring onion and red chilli.

WHAT YOU'LL NEED FROM YOUR STORE CUPBOARD

•Chinese 5 spice powder•cornflour•vegetable oil•garlic•rice vinegar•tomato ketchup•soy sauce

CRISPY SHREDDED CHICKEN

5 Ingredients

- 2 large skinless chicken breasts, cut into strips
- 1 tbsp sweet chilli sauce
- 1 red chilli, thinly sliced
- 2 spring onions, thinly sliced
- 2 tbsp runny honey

Method

1 In a large bowl, add 2 teaspoons of cornflour and a pinch of salt and black pepper. Coat the chicken strips in this mixture and set aside.

2 Heat a wok or large frying pan over a medium-high heat and add a splash of vegetable oil. Meanwhile, in another bowl, mix the sweet chilli sauce with 2 teaspoons of soy sauce, 2 teaspoons of cornflour and 75ml/2½floz of water.

3 Add the chicken into the pan in batches, frying each for 2-3 minutes, until crispy and golden. Place the chicken on kitchen paper to remove any excess oil and leave to the side.

4 Next, add some more oil into the pan and fry half of the sliced chilli and spring onion for 1 minute.

5 Pour in the honey, followed by the sweet chilli sauce mixture, and allow to simmer for 2 minutes.

6 Add the chicken into the pan and ensure it is coated evenly in the sauce.

7 Allow to simmer for a few more minutes, to heat through the chicken and thicken the sauce.

8 To serve, add to a dish straight away and scatter over the rest of the red chilli and spring onion.

WHAT YOU'LL NEED FROM YOUR STORE CUPBOARD
•cornflour•salt & pepper•soy sauce•cornflour•vegetable oil

CHICKEN WITH CASHEW NUTS

nom

5 Ingredients

- 450g/1lb skinless chicken breast, diced
- 1 egg white
- 100g cashew nuts
- 1 red bell pepper, thinly sliced

Method

1 Place the chunks of chicken into a large bowl and mix with the egg white, a teaspoon of sesame oil, 1 teaspoon of salt and 2 teaspoons of cornflour.

2 Place the bowl in the fridge and chill for 20-25 minutes.

3 Pre-heat a wok or large frying pan over high heat and add a splash of sesame oil.

4 Add in the chicken and stir frequently until cooked through.

5 Remove the chicken from the pan and place on kitchen towel to remove any excess oil.

6 In the same pan, pour in a bit more oil if needed, then stir-fry the cashew nuts and red pepper for 1 minute.

7 Next, pour in 1 tablespoon of rice vinegar and 1 tablespoon of soy sauce.

8 Add the chicken back into the wok and stir-fry for a further 3 minutes, or until heated through.

9 Serve straight away and enjoy hot.

WHAT YOU'LL NEED FROM YOUR STORE CUPBOARD
•sesame oil•salt•cornflour•rice vinegar•soy sauce

KING PRAWNS WITH BAMBOO SHOOTS

nom

5 Ingredients

- 10 tiger prawns, uncooked
- 20g/¾oz carrot, peeled and sliced
- 75g/3oz water chestnuts, drained
- 100g/3½oz bamboo shoots, sliced

Method

1 First, blanch the king prawns for a minute and the vegetables for 2 minutes, then drain.

2 Meanwhile, heat a wok over high heat and add a splash of sesame oil.

3 Add the carrot, water chestnuts and bamboo shoots to the pan, along with the oyster sauce, 1 teaspoon of soy sauce, 60ml/2floz of water, a pinch of salt and ½ teaspoon of brown sugar.

4 Reduce the heat down to a simmer and then thicken the mixture using cornflour, stirring often.

WHAT YOU'LL NEED FROM YOUR STORE CUPBOARD

•sesame oil•oyster sauce•soy sauce•salt•brown sugar•cornflour

SWEET AND SOUR KING PRAWNS

nom

5 Ingredients

- 150g/5oz fresh king prawns
- 50g/2oz onion, roughly chopped
- 75g/3oz red pepper, de-seeded and chopped
- 1 tin of pineapple
- 1 spring onion, finely sliced

Method

1 Sieve a tablespoon of cornflour into a small bowl and then pour in 1 tablespoon of water. Whisk together well and place to one side.

2 Place a wok on a medium heat and add in a drizzle of sesame oil. Add in the king prawns and cook for 3-4 minutes, stirring regularly.

3 Add in the chopped onion and pepper and stir for a further 2-3 minutes, or until the vegetables soften and the prawns are cooked through.

4 Open the tin of pineapple and drain it, keeping the juice, and chop into chunks.

5 Add the pineapple chunks and juice to the wok, along with 75ml/2½floz of rice vinegar, 75g/3oz of brown sugar, 1 tablespoon of soy sauce and 3 tablespoons of tomato ketchup, and bring to a boil.

6 Add in 1 tablespoon of the cornflour mixture and mix well.

7 Cook for 2 minutes, or until the sauce thickens, stirring occasionally.

8 Remove from the heat and serve with a sprinkling of finely sliced spring onion to garnish.

WHAT YOU'LL NEED FROM YOUR STORE CUPBOARD
•sesame oil•rice vinegar•brown sugar•soy sauce•tomato ketchup•cornflour

BEEF IN BLACK BEAN SAUCE

SERVES 4

nom

5 Ingredients

- 50g/2oz fermented black beans
- 2 inch piece of ginger, peeled and grated
- 300g/10½oz beef fillet, sliced
- ½ red chilli, de-seeded and finely chopped
- 175ml/6floz vegetable broth

Method

1 First, prepare the black bean sauce. Add the black beans, half of the ginger and 3 cloves of crushed fresh garlic to a food processor

2 Blend together until a reasonably smooth mixture is achieved. Warm a saucepan on a medium heat and add in a drizzle of vegetable oil.

3 Add in the slices of beef and cook for 2-3 minutes, stirring occasionally.

4 Add in the remaining ginger, red chilli and 2 cloves of minced garlic, and cook for a further minute.

5 Pour in the black bean mixture, along with 2 tablespoons of brown sugar, the vegetable broth, a tablespoon of rice vinegar and soy sauce.

6 Whisk the ingredients together and allow to simmer for around 8-10 minutes.

7 Meanwhile, in a bowl, whisk ¼ cup cold water with 1 tablespoon of cornflour.

8 Add into the pan and stir thoroughly just before removing the pan from the heat.

9 To serve, place on a dish and garnish by scattering over the rest of the red chilli.

WHAT YOU'LL NEED FROM YOUR STORE CUPBOARD
•vegetable oil•garlic•brown sugar•rice vinegar•soy sauce•cornflour

CRISPY ROAST DUCK

5 Ingredients

- 1 whole duck
- 4 spring onions, thinly sliced
- 1 inch piece of fresh ginger, sliced

Method

1 Preheat the oven to 170C/325F/Gas 3.

2 First, cut off and discard the flap of fat the covers the body cavity of the duck.

3 Season the duck with salt and pepper and then rub with Chinese five-spice powder. Into the cavity of the duck place 2 crushed cloves of garlic, the spring onions and ginger.

4 Place the duck on a rack over a roasting tin and cook for 1 hour, then reduce the heat to 140C/275F/Gas 1 and cook for 2½ hours, until the skin is crisp but the flesh is still tender. Once the duck is cooked, transfer onto a plate, loosely cover with foil and allow to rest for around 15 minutes.

5 To serve, use two forks to flake the meat off of the duck and place in a serving dish.

WHAT YOU'LL NEED FROM YOUR STORE CUPBOARD
•salt & pepper•Chinese 5 spice powder•garlic

CHICKEN IN LEMON AND GARLIC SAUCE

5 Ingredients

- 4 tbsp of freshly squeezed lemon juice
- 450g/1lb chicken, thinly sliced
- 100g/3½oz mangetout
- 150g/5oz bamboo shoots
- 225g/8oz tin of water chestnuts, drained

Method

1 In a large bowl, whisk together 4 freshly minced cloves of garlic, 4 tablespoons of lemon juice, 4 tablespoons of water, 2 tablespoons of soy sauce and 2 teaspoons of cornflour, and place to one side.

2 Heat a wok over high heat and add in a splash of sesame oil.

3 Add in the chicken and cook for 4-5 minutes, or until the chicken is cooked through, stirring occasionally.

4 Then, add in the mangetout, bamboo shoots and water chestnuts and stir-fry for a further 1-2 minutes.

5 Next, pour in the lemon and garlic sauce and stir-fry for around 5 minutes, or until the vegetables are tender but not overcooked, and the sauce thickens to a syrup-like consistency.

6 If required, add in a little more flour or water in order to achieve the syrup-like consistency. Season to taste with salt and black pepper just before serving.

WHAT YOU'LL NEED FROM YOUR STORE CUPBOARD
•garlic•soy sauce•cornflour•sesame oil

GINGER CHICKEN WITH BAMBOO SHOOTS

5 Ingredients

- 1 sprig of coriander, leaves and stalks separated
- 250g/9oz chicken, chopped

- 1 small knob of ginger, grated
- 6 spring onions, finely sliced
- 100g/3½oz bamboo shoots

Method

1 Add the coriander stalks, 1 tablespoon of brown sugar and 3 tablespoons of soy sauce to a food processor and blitz together.

2 Place the chopped chicken chunks into a bowl and pour the sauce all over them.

3 Place a wok on a high heat and add in a splash of sesame oil.

4 Once hot, add in the ginger, spring onions and bamboo shoots and stir-fry for 1-2 minutes, or until the beansprouts begin to wilt.

5 Pour in 1 tablespoon of soy sauce and a pinch of black pepper, stir for 1 minute, then place the contents onto a serving dish.

6 Pour a little more sesame oil into the wok and add the chicken.

7 Stir-fry the chicken, without the excess marinade, for 5-6 minutes, or until cooked through, then add the leftover marinade into the pan.

8 Once heated through thoroughly, pour over the vegetables and serve with a coriander garnish.

WHAT YOU'LL NEED FROM YOUR STORE CUPBOARD

•brown sugar•soy sauce•sesame oil•pepper

LEMON CHICKEN

nom

5 Ingredients

- The juice of 1 lemon
- 2 large chicken breasts in breadcrumbs
- 75g/3oz yellow pepper, de-seeded and finely sliced
- 75g/3oz bamboo shoots
- 2 spring onions, finely sliced

Method

1 Pre-heat the oven to 180C/350F/Gas 4.

2 In a large bowl, mix the lemon juice, 4 tablespoons of water, 2 tablespoons of soy sauce and 2 teaspoons of cornflour, and place to one side.

3 Place the chicken on a baking tray and cook in the oven for 35-40 minutes, or a little less if the pieces are smaller than the size of a full breast.

4 Meanwhile, place a wok on a high heat and add in a splash of sesame oil.

5 Add in the peppers and cook for 1-2 minutes, then throw in the bamboo shoots and most of the spring onion and cook for a further 3-4 minutes.

6 Next, pour in the prepared lemon sauce and stir-fry for 2-3 minutes.

7 The sauce should be fairly thin; add a splash of water to thin down if required.

8 Season to taste with salt and black pepper just before serving.

9 Once cooked, remove the chicken in breadcrumbs from the oven and cut into fine slices. Drizzle over the lemon sauce and vegetables, and serve with the remaining spring onions sprinkled on top.

WHAT YOU'LL NEED FROM YOUR STORE CUPBOARD
•soy sauce•cornflour•sesame oil

CONVERSION CHART: DRY INGREDIENTS

Metric	Imperial
7g	¼ oz
15g	½ oz
20g	¾ oz
25g	1 oz
40g	1½oz
50g	2oz
60g	2½oz
75g	3oz
100g	3½oz
125g	4oz
140g	4½oz
150g	5oz
165g	5½oz
175g	6oz
200g	7oz
225g	8oz
250g	9oz
275g	10oz
300g	11oz
350g	12oz
375g	13oz
400g	14oz

Metric	Imperial
425g	15oz
450g	1lb
500g	1lb 2oz
550g	1¼lb
600g	1lb 5oz
650g	1lb 7oz
675g	1½lb
700g	1lb 9oz
750g	1lb 11oz
800g	1¾lb
900g	2lb
1kg	2¼lb
1.1kg	2½lb
1.25kg	2¾lb
1.35kg	3lb
1.5kg	3lb 6oz
1.8kg	4lb
2kg	4½lb
2.25kg	5lb
2.5kg	5½lb
2.75kg	6lb

CONVERSION CHART: LIQUID MEASURES

Metric	Imperial	US
25ml	1fl oz	
60ml	2fl oz	¼ cup
75ml	2½ fl oz	
100ml	3½fl oz	
120ml	4fl oz	½ cup
150ml	5fl oz	
175ml	6fl oz	
200ml	7fl oz	
250ml	8½ fl oz	1 cup
300ml	10½ fl oz	
360ml	12½ fl oz	
400ml	14fl oz	
450ml	15½ fl oz	
600ml	1 pint	
750ml	1¼ pint	3 cups
1 litre	1½ pints	4 cups

Printed in Great Britain
by Amazon

49984089R00056